REAL-TIME PARENTING

A GUIDE FOR PARENTS

REAL-TIME PARENTING

CHOOSE YOUR ACTION STEPS FOR
THE PRESENT MOMENT

AMY ARMSTRONG | MARY FUNARI | BETH MILLER

Real-Time Parenting

A Guide for Parents: Choose Your Action Steps for the Present Moment
Amy Armstrong, Mary Funari, and Beth Miller

ISBN: 978-0-578-85483-0
Library of Congress Control Number: 2021902287

Disclaimer: Although the authors and publisher have made every effort to ensure that the information in this book was correct at press time, the authors and publisher do not assume and hereby disclaim any liability to any party for any loss, damage, or disruption caused by errors or omissions, whether such errors or omissions result from negligence, accident, or any other cause.

Real-Time Parenting

Chicago, IL

If your organization, book club, school, college, university, or community group would like to order copies of this book at a discount, and for all other inquiries, please contact www.trueparentcoaching.com

Dedicated to every parent who could use a little boost today.

A GUIDE FOR PARENTS

REAL-TIME PARENTING

CHOOSE YOUR ACTION STEPS FOR THE PRESENT MOMENT

www.trueparentcoaching.com

Preface 1

Introduction: An Invitation to Take Action 3

1. Parenting is About Parents 11

2. See the Child in Front of You 33

3. Creating Your Personal Vision 55

4. The Magic of the Parent-Child Relationship 71

5. Influencing Your Child's Behavior 91

6. Discipline Means Teaching Responsibility 111

7. Change Happens One STEP at a Time 133

8. Energizing Your Action Plan 153

References 168

Acknowledgments 173

About Us 176

PREFACE

Real-Time Parenting originated from our collaboration as three parent coaches supporting and inspiring each other. We discovered renewed energy as we listened to one another and shared our experiences and best practices in parenting. Collectively we have worked with over a thousand moms and dads through coaching, facilitating groups, teaching classes, and giving presentations. It has been an honor to guide parents to develop trust in themselves and enhance their family connections. Our passion for reaching parents continues to grow as we develop and deliver experiential activities, stories, and models for learning.

We are grateful for many tremendous guides who have led us in our work as parent coaches. The three of us received rigorous training through The Parent Coaching Institute and we continue to be inspired by the trainers who supported us to become Certified Parent Coaches®. Additionally, we learn every day from the parents we coach and those who attend our classes and workshops. It is a privilege to see the courage that flows out of parent coaching sessions and classes as parents discuss even the most tumultuous and confusing situations about children of all ages.

We are approved instructors of The Art of Positive Parenting (TAPP), a program of Action for Children in Columbus, Ohio. In the introduction to her book *The Art of*

Positive Parenting, author Mickey Tobin states that TAPP "promotes the role of the parent as the foundation of a healthy society." Tobin's course is grounded in positive communication and a democratic approach to discipline. She referenced the work of many child experts, including Haim Ginott, Thomas Gordon, Adele Faber, and Elaine Mazlish. Based on the work of these thought leaders, Tobin recognized that many parents were unaware that positive approaches for raising and disciplining their children were not only possible but also effective.

We are hopeful. We see the universality of positive approaches that are beneficial to parents everywhere. In addition, we have learned so much about how human brains work and the mind-body connection. The work and findings of Dan Siegel, Carol Dweck, Hal Runkel, Shefali Tsabary, and Marc Brackett as well as other writers, scholars, and researchers, have given us new understandings about neuroscience, motivation, positive psychology, and optimal learning environments for children. As coaches, we are fascinated by how these experts uphold and extend the practices of compassionate communication, problem ownership, positive discipline, collaborative problem-solving, and stress reduction.

Many of today's experts also extol the benefits of the ancient practice of mindfulness meditation for self-awareness and deeper connection with self and others. The focus on self-care we learned from the Parent Coaching Institute® and TAPP takes on greater depth and meaning for us today. We incorporate self-care and mindfulness in our coaching sessions and in *Real-Time Parenting*.

Most importantly, we are eternally grateful for our children who brought our identities as parents to life. Among the three of us, we have eight precious children who have unique strengths and gifts that make the world a better place. We honor our unpredictable and meaningful parenting journeys. There have been confusing and painful times as well as countless treasured and celebrated moments. As our families joyfully expand with stepchildren and grandchildren, the learning continues. We share our challenges and joys and apply *Real-Time Parenting* concepts in our family lives every day. We continue to discover beautiful insights and powerful breakthroughs in parenting. We desire to partner with you as you choose action steps for the present moment.

INTRODUCTION: AN INVITATION TO TAKE ACTION

Many parents come to us feeling dissatisfied with how they are faring as parents and discouraged with their family life. Balancing the demands of caring for children, relationships, work, and household tasks leaves everyone feeling stressed. Power struggles, busy schedules, and endless to-do lists overshadow the good times. Feelings of frustration and uncertainty sprout like weeds in place of budding satisfaction and confidence.

We know from personal and professional experience that there is no one-size-fits-all approach to raising children. While this statement may seem obvious, parents often compare themselves to perceived norms from social media, friends, other families, or cultural ideals. While an abundance of parenting resources is available, the information shows little regard for the unique needs and strengths of an individual parent or family. Parents struggle with putting clever parenting tips they read or hear into practice. They lack confidence and clarity as to what will actually create the family life they desire.

Our mission is to help you raise awareness about who you are as a parent right now and who you aspire to be at your best. As your parent coaches, we are eager to provide insight, information, resources, tools, and activities to help you clarify what matters most to you, embrace your personal strengths, and unleash your ingenuity and creativity. We invite you to connect with what is true and most important to you as you accept this invitation to choose your action steps for the present moment.

WHAT DO WE MEAN BY REAL-TIME PARENTING?

The present moment invites parents to choose authentic, effective responses to everyday challenges. Ordinary moments hold the potential for the most meaningful impact. The everyday, real interactions over spilled milk, wrestling matches between siblings, unfinished homework, and temper tantrums define the parenting experience. Intense emotions may leave you raw and reeling in the heat of the moment. Reactions don't match deeply held beliefs. These micro-moments provide opportunities to create respectful parent-child relationships.

Real-Time Parenting includes a collection of parenting skills that become your personal toolkit. These best practices are the most effective parenting responses no matter what the moment brings. We want you to make informed parenting decisions with an emphasis on the connection between parent and child that is the

hallmark of effective parenting. We include tools for productive communication and discipline strategies that propel children toward healthy independence. Our hope is that this book leads you to integrate the best, widely accepted parenting practices into the parent-child relationship that is exclusively yours.

Stress is real, but not an excuse to give up. We teach parents to look closely into the real-time experiences and needs of each family member, rather than in preconceived ideas of how parenting "should" be. No matter your circumstances, the "right" answers to parenting questions are those which are your own. *Real-Time Parenting* gives you a fresh look into what is possible for your family. Hold on to the best of what previous generations believed or practiced. Dismantle false beliefs built by the comparison culture. Take inventory of your values, personality, and experiences to craft a unique vision.

Discovering a personal parenting approach is not a one-and-done exercise. Parents learn to continually hone their parenting as children enter new developmental stages, as different circumstances arise, and as the parent-child relationship evolves. As you learn these skills, you will see how different approaches work for different parents and children in various situations. Knowing yourself and your child allows you to create the family life you most desire.

You are the author and artist creating your authentic parenting approach. We encourage you to let go of external opinions and previous conclusions when creating your optimal family life. We invite you to intentionally choose the parenting skills that best fit your goals. While we love coaching you through the process, no one can do it for you. We celebrate with you as you discover the right steps to take action today.

We don't start with how-to. We start with discovery. We can't give you specific tools until you know what you are trying to achieve and why. Six key questions help you discover insight to better understand your current situation.

WHO ARE YOU?

Chapter 1 asks you to explore how your personality, values, and past experiences may influence the action steps you choose to take. We invite you to let go of *Who should I be* and ask, *Who am I at my best*? Get to know and develop the positive beliefs and unique strengths you bring to parenting. Give your truest self to your child as a precious gift. As you embrace the beauty of your authenticity, you will begin to measure only against your best self — not to who you see on social media!

WHO IS YOUR CHILD?

Chapter 2 opens up new ways of seeing and understanding children based on your observations and learning from the field of child development. We encourage a shift from thinking, *Who should my child be?* to *Who is my child at his or her best?* *Real-Time Parenting* provides parents with a summary of best practices for optimal brain development, learning, and social-emotional growth. Additionally, we provide ways for parents to better understand what is unique about their child's traits and temperament. By understanding who their child truly is, parents can most effectively meet their child's needs.

WHAT ARE YOUR GOALS?

As you learn more about yourself and your child, you will begin to prioritize goals and create vision statements. These unfold in Chapter 3. We walk you through the process of declaring a vision of what you want to create for your parenting experience. Some families focus on academics or service, while other families prioritize creativity, community involvement, or sports.

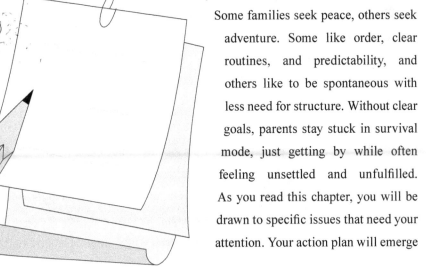

Some families seek peace, others seek adventure. Some like order, clear routines, and predictability, and others like to be spontaneous with less need for structure. Without clear goals, parents stay stuck in survival mode, just getting by while often feeling unsettled and unfulfilled. As you read this chapter, you will be drawn to specific issues that need your attention. Your action plan will emerge based on the vision statements you have for success in each area.

HOW STRONG IS YOUR RELATIONSHIP WITH YOUR CHILD?

The parent-child relationship is the basis for all significant teaching and discipline, as well as the foundation for a strong sense of belonging in the family. It's never too late to improve this connection through positive and effective communication. Chapter 4 provides practical tools for intentional listening as well as communication traps to avoid. When children feel seen and heard, they are more likely to listen to their parents in return. Trust, respect, and love are all enhanced as parents prioritize connection in everyday moments.

WHAT IS HOLDING YOU BACK?

Specific ideas for responding to everyday parenting situations fill Chapters 5 and 6. We share insight on using specific language to provide encouragement, offer choices, and give directions to boost your influence on your child's sense of self and behavior. Effective practices for setting up the physical environment, establishing routines, creating rules and consequences, and solving problems round out the toolkit. As you acquire and practice skills, you have options to fill in your action plan. In Chapter 7 we share a specific "STEP" model which helps you build awareness of your limiting beliefs, unwanted habits, and other obstacles getting in the way of your parenting. Your specific action steps will allow you to parent effectively, make important decisions, and provide a secure environment for safety, learning, and fun.

WHAT DO YOU NEED TO THRIVE?

The last discovery, revealed in Chapter 8, involves becoming aware of your energy level as a parent and the critical link between your well-being and your ability to be the parent you want to be. By embracing a positive mindset, practicing self-care, and engaging with supportive friends and community, parents find inspiration to take impactful action steps with confidence. Parents are empowered to celebrate their daily wins and let go of anxiety and doubt. Parents learn to accept the evolving parenting experience and find ways to supercharge their action plan every day.

> *Real-Time Parenting* teaches how to:
> - Embrace your authentic self
> - Tap into your most meaningful values
> - Maximize your strengths
> - Commit to self-care
> - Harness supportive resources
> - Set practical and realistic expectations
> - Meet your children and family right where they are
> - Consider best practices from current research
> - Synchronize your vision of parenting to the family you have
> - Celebrate your successes every day

HOW TO USE THIS BOOK

We understand parents are seeking relief and meaning in the parent role. This book will help you become aware of the many influences that impact your parenting, and thoughtfully choose what propels you and your family upward.

Each chapter is packed with stories based on real families we cheered on to solve their parenting challenges. You will see a movie reel to identify these stories. As you meet the moms and dads in the stories, notice if you relate to their issues or situation. Our hope is that you will see yourself in some of the stories and notice why you don't relate to others. We want you to be inspired by how others have brought their visions to life and cared for themselves along the way.

In Chapters 4, 5, and 6, we share ten parenting tools as best practices to create positive changes. Look for the TOOL ICON. These tools are options for your parenting toolkit that you will practice along the way.

Throughout the chapters, you will see Practice for Progress opportunities. Find a special notebook or device to record thoughts, questions, and ideas. Use these activities to test out approaches and experiment with skills and concepts, putting the ideas into real-time

action. See what works for you, and what doesn't. Discover what helps you achieve your vision and notice what is satisfying about it. Offer do-overs for yourself and your child. Do you need to learn more, or do you find that a particular skill is not a good fit for the situation? Keep a list of your thoughts and questions to watch your learning unfold.

Consider collaborating with a partner or support person as you reflect on the ideas and activities in each chapter. Share your thoughts and be open to insight from others. Notice your self-talk. Does it sound limiting or judgmental? Practice observing your thoughts and actions as an exercise in awareness, with the intention of learning and developing the parenting approach that gives life to your highest hopes.

Visit us online at www.trueparentcoaching.com to find support, ask questions, explore ideas, practice strategies, and discuss your progress. Sign up for a *Real-Time Parenting* class or workshop, gain insight from others, and continue your learning.

Are you ready to take action today to create positive, enduring change? Your *Real-Time Parenting* coaches are excited to support you as you discover new insights about yourself and your child, clarify your vision, test out action steps, hone your skills, and experience greater confidence and joy!

And so, the adventure begins. Go where you feel most alive.

If you want to go fast, go alone. If you want to go far, go together.

African proverb

1

PARENTING IS ABOUT PARENTS

In this chapter, we invite you to identify:

- Your unique personality traits and values
- How your own childhood may affect your parenting
- The importance of self-awareness and stress management

Does the phrase "parenting is about parents" catch you off guard? Isn't parenting about raising children? In fact, most parenting books are about addressing a child's behavior, such as handling a strong-willed child, correcting a misbehaving child, and shaping a resilient child. We take a different approach. We believe the starting point is looking **within**.

How are you doing right now? You've already taken action steps to be here reading this book. That's a big deal! It takes courage and commitment to step out of your busy life and focus on your parenting. Acknowledge your efforts and willingness to make improvements. We know parenting can be messy and gut wrenching as often as it is blissful and fulfilling, despite what your social media feed is displaying. If you are feeling low - doubting yourself or regretting past behavior

— please know it is never too late to change things for the better.

It's never too late to create a better relationship with your child and reach your parenting goals!

We invite you to discover and embrace a *Real-Time Parenting* approach that highlights your values, priorities, and the specific needs in your family situation. As you embark on this journey of self-discovery, we encourage you to keep an open mind. Frustration, confusion, worries, and missteps are a normal part of the experience. Parents often react out of emotion instead of delivering an effective, thoughtful response. You are not alone. We provide stories of real parents struggling with challenges and finding their way. A few of the stories are based on our own lives. We've been there too and want you to know we are with you now as you discover your personal action plan.

We believe in do-overs. Mistakes and corrections are part of the growth process. *Practice for Progress* is our motto. We invite you to practice with activities in each chapter. Let go of any perfectionist tendencies as you reflect on your own experiences and test out new skills and strategies. Just as musicians continually tune and practice playing their instruments, we must keep practicing and fine-tuning our parenting crafts.

BREAK FREE OF THE OLD 'CONTROLLING THE CHILD' APPROACH

Hal Runkel, relationship expert and author of *ScreamFree Parenting*, proclaims a revolutionary approach in which the focus is on the parent's behavior. This involves accepting what is realistically within a parent's control and what is not. As Runkel reminds us, we need to realize our *responsibility for ourselves* and our behavior, so we can embrace being *responsible to our children*. The challenge is to look at your actions through your child's eyes. Ask yourself, *Are my actions as a parent modeling what I want my child to learn about being a responsible and healthy adult?* Even though our children enter this world small, helpless, and completely dependent on us, it is our job to teach them to become competent and self-reliant as they grow. This involves letting go of control gradually and giving responsibility to the child as they are ready. Ultimately, the point of parenting is to work yourself out of a job as you eventually pass the baton to your adult child.

We find it liberating to break free of the old "controlling the child" method of parenting! This domineering approach was frustrating and defeating for many parents because the child's actions were truly out of their control. Sometimes an obedient child follows our direction and sometimes an independent child wants to do things her way. Our power as parents lies in the environment we create and how we respond to each child in each situation.

Would you like to let go of trying to over-power or micromanage your child? Imagine shifting your attention to where you can have a powerful impact—on yourself. Turning inward, we embark on the challenging and rewarding journey of self-discovery and growth. Jon Kabat-Zinn, a pioneer known for bringing the ancient practice of mindfulness meditation to the American medical system, says it well: "Parenting is a mirror that forces you to look at yourself. If you can learn from what you observe, you just may have a chance to keep growing yourself."

Transformational growth requires hard work. It's never easy to break away from old habits and stand in uncertainty while you consider and test out new approaches. From an emotional perspective, being responsible for ourselves as parents means meeting our own needs and not relying on our children to do so. Thus, we are the ones responsible for our own fulfillment, purpose, and self-worth.

Many parents fall into the trap of living their life through their children's lives, counting each accomplishment or failure as their own, and trying to make up for what was missing in their youth. This is an incredible burden to place on our children.

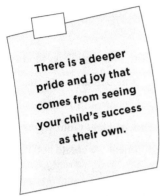

There is a deeper pride and joy that comes from seeing your child's success as their own.

Becoming a parent is an opportunity for personal growth. Responsibility for yourself means developing emotional self-regulation or grace under fire. It takes time and practice to develop the leadership skills necessary to be the voice of calm and reason our children need, especially in times of stress. Yet, this is what is required if we truly seek to be responsible to our children.

BREAKTHROUGH WITH BEDTIME

Mariana came to parent coaching with the hopes of improving bedtime with her youngest daughter, seven-year-old Julia. She was debating whether to continue the current routine of lying down and falling asleep with Julia at bedtime. She had already established a great morning ritual that was dependent on her and her daughter getting enough rest the night before. Mariana described how her exhaustion was a barrier to creating the relationships and life she wanted with her family.

One evening following their routine of reading together and cuddling, Mariana had a breakthrough when she stepped out of her comfort zone and told her daughter it was time for her to go to sleep on her own. She noted how much of this habit of staying with Julia and falling asleep with her was related to guilt she felt as a busy professional and mother of two. At the next coaching session, Mariana shared how she had claimed respect for herself and spoke with certainty. Julia responded by falling asleep and staying in her bed all night.

This experience gave Mariana confidence to improve the bedtime routine for the family. With her coach, she envisioned acting as if this new schedule was already happening. She described how it brought tremendous relief and satisfaction to her. Mariana noted when she communicates with conviction, her children sense that she is serious about creating a more structured bedtime routine. She came up with an action plan to test out for a week. Her plan included setting a timer at 8:00 p.m., dropping what she's doing, and heading upstairs to read with Julia. Marianna decided if Julia went to sleep on her own (without her mom lying down next to her) and stayed in her bed through the night for seven days, she would get to choose the family activity for the weekend.

At the next session, Mariana reported that Julia did well and slept on her own for seven nights. Julia chose mini-golf for the family activity on Saturday. However, after this successful run, Julia went right back to coming to her Mom's bed in the middle of the night. Mariana reported the trial run was good regardless because it helped her see two things: Julia could fall asleep on her own and Marianna played a part in the problem. While Mariana acknowledged this was a couple of steps forward, followed by a couple of steps backward, she made an important discovery. Changing the habit of falling asleep with Julia would be difficult for her and she had the choice to keep working on it.

THE BENEFITS OF AUTHORITATIVE PARENTING

Psychologist Diana Baumrind defined three main styles of parenting — authoritarian, permissive, and authoritative. The authoritarian style recounts a "do as I say not as I do" approach that gives children little respect or opportunity to participate in decision-making. At its worst, this style of parenting is overly controlling and can lead to broken relationships and rebellious behavior by children who refuse to obey. The other extreme parenting style, permissive parenting, is characterized by children calling the shots. Mom and Dad give in to their children's wants and wishes, sacrificing their own needs and priorities in the process. While many may think spoiled children are the result of this permissive approach, the truth is often far worse, as children feel overwhelmed with the power thrust upon them. The lack of boundaries can provoke anxiety. Finally, the balanced approach, authoritative parenting, is touted as most effective for raising children because it integrates both parental authority and child participation.

Authoritative parenting includes clear rules for safety and age-appropriate structure for daily routines, responsive interactions and loving relationships, and a mutually-respectful family environment. We agree with the best practices of authoritative parenting AND believe there is no one-size-fits-all approach to parenting.

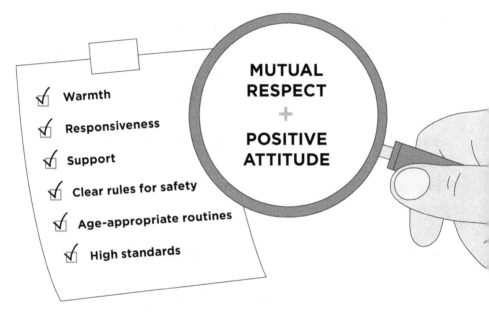

- ☑ Warmth
- ☑ Responsiveness
- ☑ Support
- ☑ Clear rules for safety
- ☑ Age-appropriate routines
- ☑ High standards

MUTUAL RESPECT + POSITIVE ATTITUDE

Consider the many families you know and the variations in schedules, activities, rules, and priorities. There are families who prioritize structure and adhere to a strict bedtime and nap schedule. They are able to let go of the fear of missing out when opportunities arise that conflict with their daily routine. And, there are families who run in a more free-form manner. These families enjoy putting spontaneity and adventure ahead of predictability. Parents use different strategies with their children, including how much direction they give, how flexible they are, and how well they collaborate. There are many ways to parent well depending on your personality, values, and family situation. We encourage you to experiment with strategies within the framework of authoritative parenting.

Two key attributes of authoritative parenting are directiveness and responsiveness. Both are important for effectively raising healthy children. Baumrind originally used the term demandingness, which may have negative connotations today. We prefer the term directiveness to describe clear expectations and boundaries around behavior. Responsiveness is demonstrating an awareness of the child's needs and meeting the needs consistently. Together, directiveness and responsiveness create a foundation of mutual respect. We encourage parents to keep these qualities of authoritative parenting in mind **and** find strategies that are comfortable and effective for them in their unique family situation.

Some parents are more relaxed in their approach and others are more structured, depending on their personality style and priorities. For example, some parents will have a set schedule for when they put their baby down for naps and will prioritize the family schedule around nap times. Other parents are less structured and open to accepting opportunities that conflict with nap time. They hope the baby will sleep in the car or stroller while they are out. While these two approaches to parenting are different, one is not necessarily right or wrong. They both fall under the umbrella of authoritative parenting. The success of each approach depends on many factors, including the child's age, temperament, and the parent's personality. In some situations, you may adopt a different approach, such as when you are on a family vacation or when your child is ill. We encourage parents to play to their strengths and be adaptable when necessary.

Young children require a greater amount of supervision and attention than older, more independent children. Yet, there are always different parenting strategies to consider. For example, when feeding a toddler, one parent may sit opposite the child and provide continual encouragement or even hold pieces of food to the child's mouth. Another parent may place the child's food on the highchair tray and sit nearby, focusing on eating her own food or having a conversation with another family member. Both parents are meeting their child's need for food. The difference lies in their level of involvement.

Sometimes, a parent's good intention to support their child goes awry. Have you heard of "helicopter parenting" and, more recently, "snowplow parenting?" These labels depict parents who are hyper-involved in their children's lives. They are overly attached to their child's accomplishments and try to remove any obstacles in the way. Yet, in doing so they rob children of learning from their own experiences and mistakes. An example is a parent who brings a high school child her homework that was left on the kitchen table or who texts the child's teacher with an excuse for why the homework was forgotten. The headlines about parents who falsified their children's college applications to selective schools is an extreme case of snowplow parenting. On the other end of the spectrum are parents who are less involved in a child's day-to-day life. An example is a child who is bored during summer vacation. A less involved parent may suggest their child go outside to play with others but will let the child figure it out. In contrast, a more involved parent may take on the child's problem as their own and offer to play a favorite game with the child or arrange a playdate.

Authoritative parenting aims to integrate parental authority and child participation. An authoritative parent allows the child to experience challenges and learn from them while providing enough support to keep the child safe and secure. As coaches, we encourage parents to check their level of involvement regularly and be open to stepping back as their child enters each new stage of development. This approach helps children become responsible, respectful, and independent.

WHAT ARE YOUR PERSONALITY TRAITS?

Have you ever taken a personality inventory for a job interview or leadership training? Your personality type reflects your in-born preferences for approaching life. It affects how you parent and how you interact with your co-parent and child. We invite you to discover your personality type to understand yourself better and to determine which parenting approaches will work best for you. We have listed key adjectives that are generally associated with different personality types. Scan through the list of words and note which words resonate with you. Add other words to the list as needed. Note and prioritize the top three words that describe your personality best. Next, repeat this exercise from a different angle: note the three words that describe your personality least.

SAMPLE PERSONALITY TRAITS		
◯ Responsible	◯ Flexible	◯ Cooperative
◯ Strategic	◯ Sincere	◯ Creative
◯ Independent	◯ Versatile	◯ Practical
◯ Perceptive	◯ Adventurous	◯ Dependable
◯ Idealistic	◯ Outgoing	◯ Spontaneous
◯ Conscientious	◯ Organized	◯ Playful
◯ Curious	◯ Diplomatic	◯ Insightful
◯ Enthusiastic	◯ Nurturing	◯ Productive
◯ Intellectual	◯ Optimistic	◯ Sensitive
◯ Logical	◯ Peaceful	◯ Supportive
◯ Compassionate	◯ Ambitious	◯ Cautious

Consider how your personality traits influence your parenting. Are there certain activities you prefer doing with your child? Would playing a card game with your teenage son bring you joy? Or, would watching him mow the lawn while you weed the flower bed bring you satisfaction? How do your personality traits influence your relationship with your spouse or partner? After you've put your child to bed, would some kind words of appreciation feel good? Or, would you prefer he clean up the kitchen so you can take a break?

WHAT ARE YOUR VALUES?

Consider the famous quote by Mahatma Gandhi:

Your beliefs become your thoughts,
Your thoughts become your words,
Your words become your actions,
Your actions become your habits,
Your habits become your values,
Your values become your destiny.

This quote highlights the formation and importance of values. We can look at different types of families from this lens. There are sports-oriented families and families who are faith-filled and religious. There are families with extended family involvement and families who operate in their own bubble. There are parents who choose to co-sleep with their infant or toddler and parents who want to have their child in his or her own crib at three months. To discover what's most important to you and your partner or spouse, we recommend beginning with a values clarification exercise. When you clarify your most important values, you allow them to permeate your actions in real time.

The following chart includes a number of value words. Please add any values that are important to you.

SAMPLE VALUES		
○ Academics	○ Caring	○ Helpfulness
○ Hobbies or passions	○ Generosity	○ Teamwork
○ Cooperation	○ Citizenship	○ Critical thinking
○ Adventure	○ Responsibility	○ Socially confident
○ Individuality	○ Independence	○ Healthy lifestyle
○ Friendship	○ Cleanliness	○ Acceptance of others
○ Artistic expression	○ Self-reliance	○ Competition
○ Manners	○ Faith	○ Fairness
○ Loyalty	○ Community service	○ Freedom
○ Athleticism	○ Courage	○ Duty
○ Nature	○ Trust	○ Hard work
○ Fun	○ Creativity	○ Curiosity

What are your most important values as a parent? What are the top three values you most want to instill in your child? Record a few sentences explaining your desire to instill each of the top three values in your child. What is important about each value? Why is it important to you? Where did this value originate in your life?

PARENTS WORKING TOGETHER

 Lauren came to parent coaching looking for support around a major life change. She had recently accepted a new full-time job with a significant commute and would start in a few months. For over a decade, she had been the primary caregiver for her two daughters, nine-year-old Sophie and eleven-year-old Allie. She had always worked part-time from home, while managing the girls' activities, caregivers, and the majority of household chores. Her husband, Seth, had maintained a full-time corporate job while the couple had been raising their daughters.

During coaching, Lauren took a closer look at her unique personality style. She teased out the following adjectives to describe herself: nurturing, compassionate, relationship-driven, independent, intuitive, creative, dedicated, and reliable. From this list, it became clear that her number-one priority was maintaining strong relationships with her daughters as she embarked on this life change. Second, she wanted to see her daughters expand their interests and self-sufficiency. Third, she wanted to collaborate more with her husband around parenting.

Next, Lauren considered what she needed to make this vision possible. She tuned into her feeling of missing the fun, easy times she used to have with her girls when they were younger. Now, as they were getting older, she often felt like the enforcer of rules and homework and was overwhelmed with all the responsibilities that went with looking after them. She realized she needed to hire a reliable after-school caregiver and delegate many of her parenting responsibilities to Seth. Only then would she be able to relax and focus on ways to keep connected with Sophie and Allie.

Lauren shifted her attention to her husband. Seth valued the girls' education. He wanted them to excel at math and be responsible individuals. He had been more hands-off in family chores and responsibilities while Lauren was working part-time from home. When asked about Seth's strengths, Lauren described him as logical, success-oriented, patient, disciplined, and a great manager. In fact, she admired his skills at hiring and mentoring his employees at work.

At the next coaching session, Lauren zeroed in on some concrete action steps and chose a few to test out. First, she would ask Seth to take the lead in hiring an after-school caregiver. Second, they would meet as a family to develop, with their daughters' input, a chore chart and monitoring system with their daughters' input. Third, Lauren would create a brief evening ritual with Sophie and Allie that would be relaxing and fun. As she talked about these steps with her coach, it became clear that self-care would be critical for Lauren as she let go of control and started trusting Seth during what could be a messy period of change. This inspired Lauren to add a fourth step. She would watch a funny video on her commute home from work to lighten her mood for the evening.

CHILDHOOD, A LOOK BACK

All of us are shaped by the conditioning of our childhood — the influence of our parents and family culture. Some people cherish childhood memories while others carry it around like unwanted baggage. Our childhood experiences significantly impact our view of ourselves. In addition, we often default to behaviors we learned from our parents. Through coaching, we encourage parents to reflect on their past and be intentional about how they want to parent.

Daniel Siegel is a renowned author, educator, and child psychiatrist. In his book, *Parenting from the Inside Out*, written in collaboration with Mary Hartzell, he explains the importance of coming to terms with childhood experiences because it affects the way parents relate to their children. Unresolved issues cause powerful emotions ranging from frustration to distress. When a parent is overwhelmed by emotion, he or she cannot be fully attentive to the child's needs. Siegel and Hartzell recommend "inner work" for parents to make sense of their past experiences and gain awareness of their reactions to stressful situations. This is not a simple or fast process for most people. It involves having an open mind, quiet reflection, revisiting past, often painful, experiences, and sharing your stories with another caring adult.

This quote from *Parenting from the Inside Out* helps explain why greater awareness on the part of the parent improves the parent-child relationship: "Self-reflection and an understanding of our internal processes allow us to choose a greater range of responses to our children's behavior. Awareness creates the possibility of choice."

HOW WERE YOU PARENTED?

Recall what stands out from your childhood. Make notes as you consider the following questions:

- How did your parents show love and care?
- Were you free to speak up as a child? Or did you fear being criticized or shamed?
- Were feelings shared and accepted in your family?
- Were there rules and structured routines?
- How were you disciplined as a child?
- How did your family resolve conflict?
- How did your parents care for themselves?

Based on these reflections, what experiences do you want to keep when parenting your child? What experiences do you want to change?

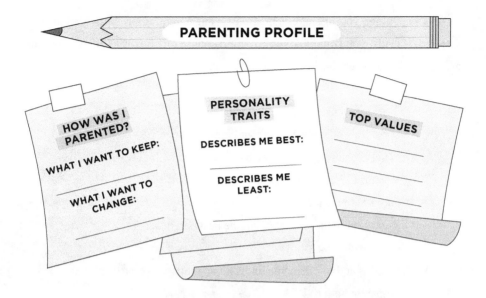

YOUR UNIQUE PARENTING PROFILE

Now that you have looked at your personality traits, top values, and how you were parented, you can combine them to form your unique parenting profile. The graphic above is an example. This self-awareness activity will guide you in understanding who you are as a parent and what matters most to you in raising your children. With greater clarity about your parenting profile, you will be able to live more intentionally and employ skills that deliver your vision for your family.

REFLECTING ON YOUR PARENTING PROFILE

Does your parenting profile represent you well or need some fine tuning? Remember you are taking a snapshot of where you are today. The goal is to understand the key influences of our parenting approach and consider what makes us unique. We all have quirks and imperfections as do our children — that's what makes us truly human. By understanding who we are as parents, we can move forward with integrity and purpose. Keep in mind, your parenting profile will change as you gain awareness and clarity about yourself and what works for you.

We encourage you to share and discuss your parenting profile with someone you trust. Ideally, you could ask your partner, spouse, or co-parent to complete the activity and take turns sharing your profiles with each other.

Below are some questions to get the conversation going.

- What do you enjoy most about being a parent?
- What is challenging for you as a parent?
- What is surprising to you in reviewing your parenting profile?
- What gets in the way of being the best parent version of yourself?
- Did this activity help you understand your spouse/partner or co-parent better?
- Did you gain any insights on how to collaborate better as parents?

WHAT GETS IN THE WAY?

Why is there a disconnect between who we truly want to be and how we show up in *Real-Time Parenting* moments? Not surprisingly, the answer is often stress. Our brains are hard-wired with a survival instinct that kicks in when we sense danger. There are three ways humans react when our primitive brain takes over — fight, flight, or freeze. For a simple explanation of the neurology behind this, we recommend viewing Siegel's "Hand Model of the Brain" on YouTube.

Certain events can flood us with negative emotions and thoughts. These events are called "triggers" because of the intense emotion and knee-jerk reaction they evoke. For example, a parent may feel anger, fear, or resentment when he sees the contents of the child's backpack spilled over the entry floor. He may think, *My son should know better*, or, *I've told him to hang up his backpack a thousand times*! He may react by yelling and/or threatening the child, "John, you careless boy. Pick this up right now or I'll take away that video game." Another parent may step over the mess, bottling up their resentment, and say nothing to the child. This parent may be unconsciously choosing to avoid conflict. Either way, the parent's powerful emotions — shown through body language, words, and actions — can be felt by a child and result in the child feeling fearful or confused. The parent's reactive behavior is not helpful in improving the problem situation.

Conversely, when a parent takes a minute or more to calm down by acknowledging the feelings and thoughts brought on by a triggering event, they are able to consider what they want the child to learn from the experience and choose an appropriate response. This skill of noticing a stress reaction and calming down, or **pausing**, is easier said than done. However, the payoff of learning to pause is powerful. We have seen many parent-child relationships change for the better because the parent implemented this skill of pausing. With continued practice, the parent can make pausing a new habit.

AN INTENTIONAL APPROACH FOR OVERWHELMING TIMES

Neha found herself without childcare during the shelter-in-place orders to slow the spread of coronavirus. Her eight-year-old son Aayan's school and after-care program were closed until further notice. Both she and her husband were working at their full-time jobs remotely. Tensions were running high as they scrambled to balance their meetings, inboxes, and deliverables while keeping up with the grocery shopping, cooking, and cleaning. Neha took on the primary responsibility of helping Aayan attend his daily virtual class with his second-grade teacher and complete his schoolwork. She came to parent coaching feeling guilty about how much she was yelling at Aayan to finish his work. She also worried about the amount of screen time her son was watching because of the lack of structured activities in his day.

During coaching, Neha took a closer look at the demands brought on by the pandemic and the amount of pressure she was putting on herself to do it all. She was overwhelmed by all the responsibilities and stress. Neha shared how much she missed just being a mom and playing with her son before bedtime. It had been months since she experienced those carefree moments. It was a relief for Neha to accept she never wanted to be an elementary school teacher or after-care counselor! She was filling in as a substitute teacher and counselor while holding down her full-time job because of the unprecedented challenges of the time. Reflecting and acknowledging these facts allowed Neha to shift her approach.

Neha decided to collaborate with her husband around Aayan's school responsibilities and free time. They agreed to alternate days helping Aayan attend class and do his work. They also decided to schedule one fun activity each day with their son that did not involve screens or schoolwork. At the next coaching session, Neha smiled as she shared how much fun she and Aayan had while making a fort in his bedroom and playing with his superheroes by flashlight.

INNER WORK IS CHALLENGING YET POWERFUL

Shefali Tsabary, clinical psychologist and parenting expert, explains how a child can have a tremendous impact and "awaken" a parent in her book, *The Conscious Parent*. "A certain child enters our life with its individual troubles, difficulties, stubbornness, and temperamental challenges in order to help us become aware of how much we have yet to grow. The reason this works is that our children are able to take us into the remnants of our emotional past and evoke deeply unconscious feelings. Consequently, to understand where our internal landscape needs to develop, we need look no further than our children's gaze."

Because of the intense emotions that may surface during introspection, it is important to move at your own pace and get the support you need from a trusted friend, relative, or a professional therapist or parent coach. Whatever your age or your child's age, it is always valuable to take time for inner work. The personal growth and awareness you gain will benefit you, your child, and your grandchildren, too. Through self-reflection and inner work, parents have the opportunity to break free of generational patterns and limiting beliefs that caused them pain as a child and raise their son or daughter differently.

Research offers hope for parents with challenging childhoods. Siegel and

Hartzell found that adults who experienced trauma or difficult conditions as a child are capable of forming a strong connection with their own child. The key to success is taking time to reflect, heal, and make sense of your past so that it does not dictate how you live in the present with your child. We do not need to stay beholden to the personal narrative we have clung to in the past. Becoming a parent is an opportunity to create a new story with you as the parent you want to be, accepting your child as he or she is here and now, in real time.

Acting differently requires thinking differently. There are always other perspectives to consider. This is why many people can witness the same event and take away different experiences. Consider the finalists of a reality show waiting to see who has been cut and who remains in the contest. Those who are cut have varied reactions based on their perspectives — some may be devastated at the loss while others may be amazed at just how close they came to winning. It always depends on how you view and interpret a situation. Put another way, our perspective shapes our thoughts and our thoughts shape our behavior. Through increased self-awareness, you can see possibilities for change as you shift from automatic thoughts and reactions to more responsive, intentional behaviors.

Becoming a parent is an opportunity to create a new story with you as the parent you want to be.

DEFINING MOMENT

Elizabeth shared a defining moment that changed the course of her life and approach to parenting. It occurred when her son Robbie was just three years old and working with an early intervention specialist, Dana, at their home. Dana was working with Robbie on communication and behavior skills. Elizabeth observed as Dana prompted and guided Robbie against his will in washing his hands before snack time. Robbie was crying and struggling to get free from the task and Elizabeth could see the fear in his eyes when he looked at her. In her words, "In that instant when our eyes met, I became acutely aware of my anxiety and strong desire to rescue him from the torment of being trapped at the small powder-room sink. I felt an ache in my core watching his despair; he saw me standing there without doing anything to help. I forced myself to turn away so I wouldn't run to him. While I did everything in my power to stay out of the unfolding drama, I was certain my expression of agony gave me away."

This was the moment Elizabeth realized she needed to come to terms with her own anxiety if she truly wanted to be the mom Robbie needed — one who could remain calm, confident, and consistent in following through with the recommended therapy. The anxiety she had pushed down inside herself since childhood could no longer be ignored. Her aversion to conflict stemmed from memories of intense family arguments growing up. Since then, she always tried to play the peacemaker. Over the years, she had talked to a therapist and taken a stress reduction course, but never committed to creating any new habits. This time was different because she saw how her reaction directly affected her son. She started with a new therapist and followed his recommendations. She also began spending more time on her yoga mat. In her words, "My love for my child propelled me to address my own anxiety and regain my well-being."

Self-care is not selfish. It is essential for parents to take care of themselves and get support when needed. An overwhelmed or exhausted parent is too depleted to care for a child. Consider the metaphor of a car's gas tank. When it is running low, we stop and refuel. Parents also need to practice activities that refill their tanks, so they aren't running on fumes.

Be compassionate with yourself as you delve into where you are today and where you want to be tomorrow. When we slow down our worried minds and focus on the present moment, we can see how stress and our reactions often lead to arguments and power struggles with our children. There is a more authentic and rewarding approach for you. As your coaches, we are here to help you bring forth your best self in *Real-Time Parenting.*

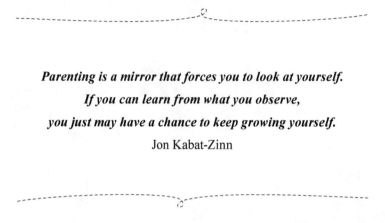

Parenting is a mirror that forces you to look at yourself.
If you can learn from what you observe,
you just may have a chance to keep growing yourself.
Jon Kabat-Zinn

---- 2 ----

SEE THE CHILD
IN FRONT OF YOU

In this chapter, we invite you to think about:

- The preferences and traits that best describe your child
- The optimal environment for your child's development
- The expectations that are most appropriate for your child's developmental stage

Who is this person you call your child? What makes her tick? What motivates, inspires, and energizes this unique human being? From the moment of birth, parents influence the beliefs a child has about herself. Parents are the springboard from which a child develops a sense of being lovable, capable, and needed.

Children are born with unique temperaments that necessitate complementary care. Even though parenting is really about the parent, parenting is only effective when parents have appropriate expectations and skills for interacting positively with their child. With careful observation and attention to the specific characteristics and development of each child, parents can provide the maximum support for the child to reach his full potential.

Whether you view your child now as a treasure or as a diamond in the rough, this chapter is about discovering the natural beauty and brilliance of your child so that you can be instrumental in helping your child shine. Just as diamond cutters examine the most effective ways to expose the worth and value of the precious stone, you can recognize the features that will bring about your child's brightest sparkle and create rewarding experiences. In the words of Chris Lee, motivational trainer, "We are all diamonds, and knowing so gives life meaning and purpose."

We encourage you to discover an approach to parenting that fits the child in front of you in real time, moment by moment. Parents create realistic expectations when they consider the inborn temperament of the child along with the child's stage of cognitive, emotional, social, physical, and moral development. In short, this chapter is about getting to know the child you have and creating the environment and interactions that most completely meet the needs of your one-of-a-kind child.

MANAGING EXPECTATIONS

When parents are not in tune with realistic expectations, they may struggle and butt heads with their children. Even the most routine events such as getting out the door in the morning or having a meal together can create power struggles and verbal battles. Other times parents experience anxiety, not knowing the right decisions regarding education, activities, or chores. Jeannie, a conscientious and somewhat anxious mother of Andrew, age eight, realized she was over-managing her son's morning routine. They were able to start their day much more smoothly when Jeannie realized Andrew was capable of getting his belongings packed for school the night before.

Joe came to coaching yearning for less chaos in his home where he lived with his wife and kindergarten twins. He preferred a methodical approach to his day and wanted the twins to keep their room neat morning and night. When Joe reviewed his expectations with his coach, he realized he had been pushing the twins to clean their room to his personal standards for neatness without providing support and direction. Joe created a new routine where he and the twins organize toys and put away clothes together. Instead of leaving the children in their room where they would inevitably end up creating even greater disarray, Joe made a habit of staying close by and giving brief, specific instructions for creating order.

PARENTING *THIS* CHILD

 Cyndi, a thirty-four-year-old high-energy executive, was very active in her work community as well as her neighborhood. She often attended meetings in the evenings and liked to participate in dinners and outings with other families. Her husband, Mark, typically enjoyed accompanying Cyndi at these events, especially if some of his best buddies were there. Mark and Cyndi's six-year-old son, Justin, tended to get disruptive in groups and turned into a bit of a bully around other children. Cyndi and Mark were often embarrassed and got angry with Justin for his disruption at gatherings. Cyndi came to coaching to see what she could do to get Justin to behave more cooperatively with the other children.

As Cyndi progressed in coaching, she realized a few things about Justin that were important factors in determining her action steps. First of all, Justin had never been much of a solid sleeper. He woke up by 4:30 a.m. or 5:00 a.m., and rarely fell back to sleep. Justin often seemed half-asleep at the dinner table and started to get cranky if he is was up past 7:00 p.m. His parents encouraged Justin to sleep in a little later in the mornings, but he was simply an early bird. Also, Justin liked a high degree of structure and predictability in his schedule, unlike his parents. Cyndi and Mark wished Justin could enjoy being around other families, staying out with them later in the evenings, and playing spontaneously with other children. As much as they tried, they could not get through an evening of activity without Justin becoming combative and disrespectful.

Coaching helped Cyndi develop an acceptance of Justin's temperament and preferred sleep patterns. She realized she was simply expecting too much from Justin, especially when he was tired. Cyndi and Mark experimented with packing a "party bag" to take to events with quiet activities for Justin. Cyndi committed to checking on Justin frequently and reminding him she was there to help him problem-solve any issues that arose. Additionally, Cyndi adjusted her expectations and schedule to either get a babysitter for Justin or be sure to bring Justin home by 8:00 p.m., even though she would prefer to stay out until 9:30 or 10:00 p.m. While this time was still a challenge for Justin, they managed well enough in real time to have fun and create good memories enjoying social and community activities as a family. The parents changed their expectations based on a new understanding of the actual traits of their child. They found new ways to support Justin and adjusted their schedule based on what worked for the entire family, which resulted in more enjoyable outings for everyone.

RESIST LABELING CHILDREN

Take a moment to look at how we think about and describe children. Imagine a neighborhood playground of four-year-old children, and a parent is describing them to a new neighbor: "Oh, that's Jack, he is the shy one. He just stays at the bottom of the slide watching the other children play. And that's Jolie over there, the one who is always bossing the other kids around. And where's Oliver? He is the one in the dirt; the more dirt he gets on his clothes, the happier he seems to be!" And when seeing the group of middle-school children waiting for the school bus, she says, "There is Raul, he is always the first in line but hardly says a word to anyone else. He must have skipped his lunch to make sure he wasn't late. And Jess, the studious, lanky girl who is a foot taller than everyone and looks like she is in

tenth grade. Lexi stands with her hip sticking out like she is modeling for a fashion magazine with lipstick and an attitude to match. Oh, and there are Nick and Derrick who are always at each other; they can't spend ten minutes together without getting into a wrestling match."

How do the descriptions above set expectations and create positive or negative judgments about these children? What do you notice about your opinions of "right" and "wrong" for how children should behave? How do any of your own values come into play when you notice your reactions to any of these or other descriptions about children? Our minds are designed to make judgments about what we observe in people. We classify information so it is organized in our brain and makes sense to us. Can we be aware of any judgments we declare about children and the impact our opinions may have on a child's identity?

Negative or limiting labels can be devastating to a child's self-image, leaving a child to think he or she is not important, does not belong, or can never achieve or behave in ways that don't match the assigned label. Can you imagine the potential side-effects for a child who is called the "class clown," a "picky eater," or the "messy one?" What about the pressure and limitations put on a child who is the "perfect student" or the "responsible one?" What would you say to describe your own child? What words do you use to compliment or brag about your children? What language do you use to criticize or complain about your children?

IMPACT OF A LABEL

 Liz, now 48, described being a straight-A student who did her household chores and homework without being reminded. She told her coach how sad she felt that she had missed out on fun activities. She did not take risks for fear of letting down her parents, who consistently described her as the "responsible one" in the family. Her parents may have been proud of her, but unknowingly gave Liz the idea she was only valuable as a model student. Liz spent all her time being meticulous with school and household tasks, rarely engaging in new activities she may have wanted to try. She developed perfectionism and felt her family never truly understood her.

Chad, a freshman in college, told of the unbearable pressure he has felt ever since being put in advanced math classes in fifth grade. He believed being categorized as the "smart kid" meant he would be a failure if he did not attend a prestigious engineering program at a prominent university. On the contrary, Kylie felt embarrassed being called a "slow reader" by a teacher who pulled her out of regular classes for testing as part of her ADHD accommodations. She felt paralyzed to speak up in class because of the label. While labels can be helpful for getting needed resources, these examples show what can happen when children are seen **only** by their label. Children (and adults!) do best when their whole self is valued and fully seen.

Can we learn to notice our judgments and avoid labels?

GET TO KNOW YOUR UNIQUE CHILD

In his book, *Brainstorm*, Dan Siegel says, "Treat people as if they were what they ought to be and you help them become what they are capable of being." How do you know who your child is capable of becoming? How is aptitude and potential determined? It is ultimately up to children to grow and develop their own ideas of what defines their best self. In the meantime, you can be open-minded to the unlimited possibilities of your child today and all he or she may become in the future.

One of our heartfelt objectives in writing *Real-Time Parenting* is to show parents ways to synchronize parenting behaviors to the child's specific combination of traits and needs. Be curious and notice what is most motivating, inspiring, and meaningful to your child. Adapting our parenting means learning how to challenge, nurture, and guide your child in a way that does not sabotage the splendor and value of their individuality. Would you say, "I can't believe how different my two children are, coming from the same parents?" If so, you are on the right track to accepting the uniqueness of your children.

TEMPERAMENT INFLUENCES BEHAVIOR

One approach to understanding differences in how children behave is looking at the child's temperament, or what is called behavioral style by researchers Alexander Thomas and Stella Chess. Temperament refers to the set of traits that organize the child's approach to his or her surroundings, such as being outgoing and adventurous, or shy and cautious. These traits are the basis for the child's developing personality and are often present at birth. As parents take a closer look at the traits of their child, they discover ways to thoughtfully structure the child's environment and align care for the child. The child's personality continues to develop with the influence of both nature (genetics) and nurture (environment and relationships).

OBSERVING YOUR CHILD

 Based on their research, Thomas and Chess described the following traits found in children that make up your child's temperament. Where does your child fall on the spectrum for each trait?

TEMPERAMENT TRAITS

1) Activity Level

Is the child always moving and doing something or is the child more often in an observant and relaxed state?

Very Active ———————— Moderately Active ——————— Not Very Active

---

2) Regularity

Does the child have regular eating and sleeping habits or are they somewhat unpredictable?

Regular Habits ——————— Semi-Regular Habits ——————— Unpredictable

---

3) Approach/withdrawal

Does the child approach new situations and new people with eagerness or tend to shy away?

Jumps Right In ——————— Moderately Eager ——————— Keeps to herself

---

4) Adaptability

Does the child adjust to changes in routines or plans easily or does the child become cranky or confused around transitions?

Adjusts Easily ——————— Moderately Adaptable ——————— Prefers Predictability

---

5) Intensity

Does the child react strongly to situations, either positively or negatively, or does the child react calmly and quietly?

Intense Reactions ———— Moderate Reactions ———— Mild Reactions

6) Mood

Does the child often express a negative outlook or is the child generally a positive person? Does the child's mood shift frequently or is the child usually even-tempered?

Even & Positive ———— Moderate ———— Changing & Negative

7) Persistence

Does the child give up quickly when a task becomes difficult or does he/she keep on trying? Can the child stick with an activity for a long time or does the child get bored or frustrated quickly?

Persists ———— Moderately Persistent ———— Quits Quickly

8) Distractibility

Does the child get easily distracted from an activity or can the child shut out distractions and stay focused with the current activity?

Focused ———— Moderately Focused ———— Distracts Easily

9) Sensory Threshold

Is the child bothered by loud noises, bright lights, or food / clothing textures, or does the child tend to ignore them and go with the flow?

Sensitive ———— Moderately Sensitive ———— Not Sensitive

UNDERSTANDING YOUR OBSERVATIONS

What if you accepted your child's uniqueness simply as information rather than praising a specific trait or merely tolerating it? While some features of a child's behavioral style are more or less convenient, comfortable, and fun to be around, accepting a child's temperament is central to accepting the child. Would you rather be around a child who is highly energetic, talkative, and embraces a variety of new experiences,

> Understanding the defining traits of a child's temperament helps parents interpret the child's behavior.

or a child who is cuddly, reserved, and content to stay at home? Neither the child nor the parent chooses the child's temperament. However, a parent's response greatly influences the child's behavior over time. Parents can learn to anticipate and either avoid or adapt to situations that might be particularly difficult for the child or parent.

Seeing and responding to the child may look different for every parent. For example, the parents of Lucy, age four, brought headphones to the Fourth of July fireworks knowing Lucy was sensitive to loud noises. Lucy could enjoy the bright colors without crying and hiding her head under the blanket. Damien, age five, was set to play at the playground with his two cousins when the weather dictated they stay home. Damien spent most of the afternoon crying, frustrated about the change, and begging to go the playground. Instead of insisting Damien quit wailing with disappointment, Damien's father understood Damien needed predictability. He gave Damien art supplies to draw pictures of all the things he wanted to do at the playground as soon as the weather cleared up.

The ways of describing children's traits, behavior and personalities are as endless as the factors that influence them. Our hope is for parents to seek to understand the child in front of them, and accept the child **first**, before deciding on action steps for parenting.

WHEN INDIVIDUAL PREFERENCES CONFLICT

In addition to temperament, it is important to notice your child's preferences. Take a closer look at your child's likes and dislikes. You will see children lean toward their favorite textures, tastes, smells, sounds, and sights. They gravitate toward particular people, activities, or interests as they respond to varied experiences.

What is it like for a parent if the child's preferences differ from their own? Consider a father whose favorite time of the year is NCAA "March Madness," but his son prefers rap music to basketball. Or a social child who can't get enough play time among friends, yet his solitary dad believes the best place for a boy is out fishing. Or what about a single mother who prioritizes academic achievement, yet her four sons prefer video gaming? Or what is a religious family to do with a twelve-year-old girl who doesn't want to go to service? And can you imagine the discord in a quiet, low-key family of introverts when the new baby in the family becomes a talkative youngster who relentlessly asks questions?

We have coached many parents who have successfully wrestled with the needs of the individual child as part of the whole family. We have had the joy of watching them integrate all family members' interests and find meaningful ways to accommodate everyone's needs respectfully.

EMBRACING THE ENGINEER

 Leo, an eight-year-old boy, loved all things mechanical. He and his best friend, Roberto, played indoors, building Legos or mastering video games. Leo resisted playing in the neighborhood like so many other boys his age. Leo did not have a favorite sports team or outdoor game. He showed an interest in playing chess and strategic board games but did not want to ride his bike or swim at the community center down his street. While Leo didn't fuss when asked to wash dishes, he complained about taking the family dogs outside and walking to the bus stop.

Leo's mom and dad, however, were avid hikers. When Leo was just a baby, they put him in a baby-pack and had him trolling around outside with them. Both parents love nature and could name most of the species of birds seen hopping about in the park in their neighborhood. They invested a lot of time and effort in exercising the family's two cocker spaniels, and planned vacations around exploring state parks.

Leo's four-year-old sister loved to play outside and had an affinity for swimming. She constantly asked to go in the water and put on her bathing suit most weekends in the hopes of going for a swim. So where did Leo fit in with this active, nature-loving family? How could he develop his passion for mechanics and computers, when his family was out at the park? How could Leo's parents demonstrate unconditional love and acceptance of him, when they didn't share the same interests? Wasn't it important for Leo to learn to participate in the family values of nature and physical activity? And wasn't it necessary for Leo to move his body in order to be physically healthy?

Working with their parent coach, Leo's parents discovered the importance of embracing Leo's individuality, and came up with a plan to embrace and integrate Leo's interests into the whole family. They allowed Leo to bring books and science activities with him to the park. While one parent played with Lucy, the other parent got a lesson from Leo in the mechanics of circuitry or some other engineering concept.

COMPARING BEHAVIOR PATTERNS IN REAL TIME

 How is your child like you? How is your child not like you? Fill in the blanks with a description of your own behavior patterns, and those of your child. Using a scale of 1-10, rate how similar or different you and your child are in each area: 1 is very similar and 10 is very different.

What most surprises you about any of your behavior patterns? Did you learn anything about yourself or your child by going through this exercise? Do any of these categories seem more significant to you? This exercise is meant to build awareness of how you see yourself in relation to your child. You are two separate individuals united in a very special parent-child relationship.

BEHAVIOR PATTERN COMPARISON

Behavior Pattern	You	Your child	Rating
BEST TIME OF DAY Morning person? Night?			
SOCIALIZATION Alone time? Prefers people?			
PHYSICAL TOUCH Closeness? Space?			
ORGANIZATION Neat? Messy?			
FOOD Bland? Spicy? Salty? Sweet? Crunchy? Soft?			
APPETITE Eats small meals frequently? Eats fewer large meals?			
SLEEP HABITS Heavy? Light?			
MOOD Silly? Serious? Steady? Varying?			
RISK TAKING Adventuresome? Observer?			
BOUNDARIES Rule follower? Rebellious?			
CONFLICT Competitive? Avoidant?			

CONSIDER THE CHILD'S DEVELOPMENTAL STAGE

Another important factor to consider when observing children in real time is their developmental stage. Children progress over time through stages that manifest in physical, social, emotional, and intellectual ways. The Bright Futures Guidelines of the American Academy of Pediatrics (AAP) reminds us that understanding child development is a central key to the care of children. When parents understand typical development, they are more able to set realistic expectations for behavior and attend to the child's health and safety needs.

"Development" refers to the stages of growth of the whole child — the child's physical body, brain, and biology, including the development of language, social connections, emotions, and intellect. Children transition through specific developmental stages as they grow from a newborn, infant, toddler, preschooler, school-age child, pre-adolescent, adolescent, and finally a young adult. These stages define normal development for healthy children. Each stage of development is marked by observable behaviors referred to as milestones. Along with many other reliable resources, the AAP provides articles and charts specific to the milestones of development for children at all ages and stages. While comparing your child's development to the developmental charts, tune in to any particular growth areas that may need to be addressed with a qualified health care provider.

It takes time as well as a fertile environment for the brain and body to grow and develop normally. Children cannot be tutored, pressured, or hurried to advance through developmental stages. Parents often mistakenly think once their child is on track with a task or skill, it is checked off the list. Conversely, worried parents sometimes assume that if the child is off track, the problem will only intensify. Rather than thinking of growth and development as a linear process, consider it more of a zigzag and a few loops in a general upward direction. You will be able to observe development in waves. Growth will manifest in new behaviors as the brain re-wires with new learning practiced over time.

Because development is complex and non-linear, it is important to view your child as a work in progress. When parents have unrealistic expectations for their children they often end up disappointed. Experimenting with new expectations and communication is essential for parents to meet the changing needs of the family. We encourage parents to use hindsight, reflection, and second chances.

MOTHER'S DAY DO-OVER

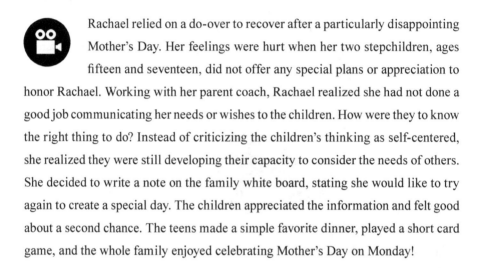 Rachael relied on a do-over to recover after a particularly disappointing Mother's Day. Her feelings were hurt when her two stepchildren, ages fifteen and seventeen, did not offer any special plans or appreciation to honor Rachael. Working with her parent coach, Rachael realized she had not done a good job communicating her needs or wishes to the children. How were they to know the right thing to do? Instead of criticizing the children's thinking as self-centered, she realized they were still developing their capacity to consider the needs of others. She decided to write a note on the family white board, stating she would like to try again to create a special day. The children appreciated the information and felt good about a second chance. The teens made a simple favorite dinner, played a short card game, and the whole family enjoyed celebrating Mother's Day on Monday!

DEVELOPING LIFE SKILLS

While much of learning takes place at school, the skills that support overall well-being extend far beyond the classroom. Incorporating chores into the daily routine of family life builds discipline, a sense of belonging in the family, and an ability to contribute in meaningful ways. Young children can help pick up toys and books, throw away trash, set the table, and help with pets. As children enter elementary school, they develop important life skills when given additional responsibilities such as cooking, cleaning, yard work, or babysitting. As you take a closer look at your children, think of the ways you can build their capabilities through contributions at home.

Bo, age thirteen, became sulky and irritable during the three months of shelter-in-place orders of the coronavirus pandemic. He missed skateboarding with his friends and complained of boredom. Bo's father noticed Bo was distraught without his normal routine and gave Bo the responsibility to help paint the back of the house. While Bo grumbled at first, he soon found that the time learning a new skill gave him something to do to pass the day, and he became proud of his work. Even though he continued to miss his buddies, he had something to brag about when they finally reconnected at the skate park.

TEACHING RIGHT FROM WRONG

Just as parents have varying values and priorities, parents have a variety of definitions for what it means for a child to be good, or to become a good person. Often, when parents describe a baby or young child as good, the parent is saying she is easy-going and goes to sleep without much fuss. For older children, good has the connotation of ethical behavior, such as staying out of trouble and being helpful around the house or with younger siblings.

According to Thomas Lickona, author of *Raising Good Children*, being good does not mean a child can never question what the child is told to do. Lickona suggests being good includes "being fair, honest, and trustworthy; being responsible for their own behavior; following legitimate authority, rules and laws; feeling a decent measure of concern for fellow human beings; being able to stand on their own feet and resist pressure to go with the crowd; and being capable of generosity and love." Teaching goodness has changed over the years — respect has replaced fear as a primary tool for teaching children right from wrong.

Licona references the stages of moral development first identified by psychologist Lawrence Kohlberg. These stages incorporate both social and intellectual learning. Each stage represents an important building block toward a healthy adaptation of social norms as the child evolves in what he views as right and why he should be good. A child's compliance with authority unfolds as parents lovingly resist power struggles and gradually promote independent play and thinking. Even though temperaments vary, every child starts out being oriented toward their own wants and needs, and over time learns to care about the feelings and rights of others.

We hope it is good news to learn children do not have to meet adult standards to be on track in their development toward becoming a mature, disciplined, and altruistic adult. Mutual respect relies on accurate expectations of how being good is manifested in each stage. At an early stage, they may do the right thing to avoid punishment, whereas at a later stage, they do the right thing to uphold their value system or support human rights. Just as children have to learn to walk before they can run, they first have to develop a strong self-interest before they can offer respect and compassion to others.

Children vary significantly with the ages they enter each stage of moral development. Generally speaking, preschoolers are primarily ego-centric, claiming that whatever they want is "mine." Then children enter a stage of unquestioning obedience that lasts through early elementary grades. Next, they shift back toward self-interest, wanting to treat people fairly based on who has shown fairness to them. By middle school through the early teenage years, they have begun developing their inner conscience, but are largely focused on social approval for their moral decisions. It is not until later teen years and into young adulthood that they can see the broader impact of their choices and support the interests of others in their community and world.

We see many parents who get upset when their expectations are not met, only to realize their expectations didn't match their child's current stage of development. For example, Stella came into a session fearful about her four-year-old son's lies regarding simple things such as finishing his milk or putting his banana peel in the trash. Through coaching, Stella was relieved to learn that at age four, "lying" could simply mean the child wishes something to be true (this is mine) or is afraid of getting punished (I did not eat the cookie). Stella realized lying wasn't as problematic for her child as she originally thought; he was simply acting out of an early stage of moral decision making. Stella found simple ways to encourage growth and correct her son without criticizing or shaming him.

HEALTHY ENVIRONMENTS FOR BRAIN GROWTH

It is important for children to engage in a variety of experiences every day for healthy brain development. Siegel teamed up with David Rock to offer the "Healthy Mind Platter," a valuable resource for parents to structure a healthy-brain environment for their children. Siegel and Rock wisely advise parents to provide seven different kinds of activities every day including down time to relax, focus time to work toward goals, sleep time to let the body recharge, creative play time to engage in new experiences, connecting time to nurture relationships, physical time to move the body, and time-in to reflect on inner feelings, images, and thoughts. With both challenging activities and nurturing support, as well as a healthy brain environment, the child will be at his or her personal best for learning, playing, and growing.

SCREENS AND MACHINES

A key environmental factor for optimal growth is providing a three-dimensional setting in which two-dimensional screens are not a primary source of entertainment. Neuroscientists and other researchers find that screen over-use sabotages healthy relationships and can leave children feeling anxious and insecure for many reasons, including:

- Screen use does not elicit normal empathy that is inherent with in-person relationships.
- Approval-seeking on social media often reinforces a consumer-based comparison culture rather than self-satisfaction of authentic expression.
- Online websites and apps can expose children and teens to dangerous and provocative content. Children are fed images and information beyond their ability to process, and at its worst, this puts children at risk with dangerous predators.
- Screen time can replace healthy critical thinking, creativity and problem-solving that comes from free play with three-

dimensional materials.

- Screens keep children indoors rather than getting fresh air and interacting with nature.
- On-screen communications can give children an opportunity to bully or be bullied as users do not see or feel the intense impact and consequences of the interactions.

The AAP recommends no screen time at all for children under eighteen months except video chatting. For older toddlers and young children, the AAP recommends parents and children watch media programs together. Many tools and resources are available for parents to closely monitor screen use and prevent inappropriate content from appearing on the child's screen. However, we hear a lot about three obstacles to healthy screen use from frustrated parents. First, technology changes daily. It's hard to keep up! Second, parents struggle to model boundaries or healthy choices regarding their own media use. And third, it takes time and skill to develop a thorough, working plan for monitoring technology use that suits the needs of all family members.

As with all parenting situations, effective plans align with the abilities, preferences, and habits of all involved. The best media usage plan for each family is the plan they can follow. Careful media use is just one example of how parents can create optimal environments for children and healthy brain development.

IT'S ABOUT THE GROWTH, NOT THE GRADE

We often hear parents want their children to "do their best" or "reach their full potential." Parents ask us, "So how do I know when my child is doing his best?" Or, "What do I do when my child is NOT doing her best?" The answers do not lie in nagging, punishing, pleading, or reminding. As we work with parents, we listen for what we can know about the parent, and what can be known about the child. We coach parents to take small steps toward understanding what they can do to support the child's development, and what helps the child feel inspired and motivated to learn and grow in positive ways.

It is all too tempting for parents to compare the development of one child to another. What parent doesn't want their child to be at the top of the pack when it comes to walking, talking, or counting to ten? While parents can certainly feel proud when their child sleeps through the night or uses the toilet regularly, earns top honors or is awarded an athletic scholarship, the ultimate parenting satisfaction depends on creating the benchmarks that best serve the individual child in real time.

As a parent, are we not to dream of what we would enjoy seeing in our child? Of course, we may create a positive vision of our child's future. At the same time, can we be aware of the expectations that spring out of our own fantasies? Let us be mindful that while our expectations can be a springboard for the child to dream big, they can also impair our ability to safeguard the very uniqueness that makes our child who she truly is. With a willingness to understand, accept, and accommodate each child's uniqueness, the family culture can be meaningful and inclusive of all family members.

Family culture can be meaningful and inclusive of all family members.

Knowing your child means knowing his heart, mind, abilities, traits, preferences, and developmental stage. Once we learn to observe and embrace the child's unique makeup, we can find ways to connect and stimulate growth through the changes in parenting that will best fit each child. Let us quiet ourselves to listen to all that lies beneath the surface and get to know our child well.

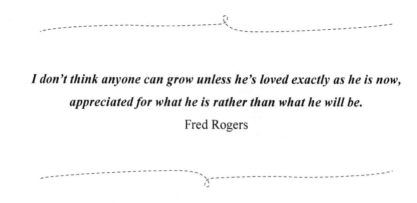

I don't think anyone can grow unless he's loved exactly as he is now, appreciated for what he is rather than what he will be.

Fred Rogers

3

CREATING YOUR PERSONAL VISION

In this chapter, we invite you to:

- Define success for your family
- Take inventory of your parenting as it is today
- Create personal vision statements to prioritize change

How do parents know when they are parenting well? What is success as it relates to parenting? As coaches, we have seen many parents crumble with the guilt and pressure they put on themselves to do it right. Even if parents know that parenting is no place to try to achieve perfection, they can be plagued by attempts to rush development and learning to keep up with perceived societal expectations. Too often they attempt to achieve a set outcome that denies the reality of their situation. Nonstop input from social media, commercialism, other parents, and extended family can create a comparison culture that sabotages parents' trust in their own judgment and inner wisdom.

When it comes to you and your child, we encourage you to explore and embrace your individual definition of success, knowing there is not one right way to be an authoritative parent. You will determine your own right parenting steps as you notice what is most energizing and confidence-building for you. We often ask, "What is working?" as a way of identifying parents' perspectives of what is right. We are here to support you in crafting specific action steps that are in alignment with your parenting profile, the specific needs of your children, and your desires for the family as a whole.

VISIONING

Without a clear, personal vision, parents end up in survival mode, just going through the motions of making reactive decisions. *Real-Time Parenting* means making choices that break through any limited thinking and unhelpful expectations parents hold about parenting. Parental self-doubt is replaced

> Parents are energized and empowered once they have specific vision statements.

with confident vision statements that are personal, informed, and inspired.

Vision statements represent your version of what success will look like. One parent may measure success by how orderly the house remains and how thoroughly tasks are accomplished. Another parent may measure success by how close and connected that parent feels to the child — how open and communicative the child is with the parent. Yet, another parent may evaluate their parenting role by the level of achievement by the child in their grades, religion, sports, activities, or citizenship. Another possible measure is how cooperative the child is to the parent's directives — or how boldly, creatively, politely, or logically the child expresses herself. These examples reflect the beliefs and values of the parent regarding what is most natural or important to them.

As coaches, it is gratifying to see parents ignite their personal passion for parenting. Rather than setting goals **for** parents, we use the visioning process to guide parents to find their own words to best describe their highest ideals for their child and family. This vision taps into the parents' deepest longings for their children, and recognizes it is in each parent's power to match his or her desires with an action plan. By learning to declare and deliver a personal and specific vision for family life, parents are energized and empowered. They trust themselves, relax more, and have an inner sense of knowing they are on the right track.

VISIONING BEGINS WITH ACCEPTANCE

Recognizing and accepting your feelings in the present moment is critical when considering what you want to create for the future. All feelings are essential information — positive and negative. Resistance creeps in when feelings are uncomfortable, yet the discomfort can be a catalyst for positive change. Lean in. Allow the feelings to come and go as important information for your vision.

While many people feel despair when things don't go as they hoped, allowing all feelings can turn frustration to insight. Even difficult moments can be a catalyst for good things to come as parents create their desired vision. Rick Hanson, clinical psychologist and author of *Resilient*, reminds us that we can take a small step back to notice difficult emotions and recognize our power to choose more of what we want. It is our biology and conditioning that naturally send signals of anxiety or defeat, yet we can re-wire our brains to create more pleasurable experiences. Visioning and breathing into what we want does just that.

When parents are sleep-deprived and overwhelmed with a new baby, they can envision feeling more rested. Moms and dads miserable with worry and resentment in the throes of adolescence may imagine moments of comfort and mutual respect. Accepting our feelings in present circumstances jumpstarts the visioning process.

THE RELUCTANT BASEBALL MOM

Rita, a school psychologist, came to coaching with her husband, Ralph, a patent attorney. Together, they had three boys who celebrated the start of baseball season as though it was the first rain after a six-month drought. Rita had many ideas about what it meant to be a good mother, including being very involved in her children's activities. Ralph and the boys watched baseball on TV or played baseball video games any day the boys didn't have their own ball games. Rita preferred artistic endeavors instead of being a passive spectator on the baseball field. She also mourned the loss of her dream of parenting a girl; Rita miscarried at twenty weeks after an ultrasound revealed she was pregnant with a girl. Rita longed for the mother-daughter experience she would never have.

As Rita worked with her parent coach, she found a broader perspective. Rather than just thinking about baseball as a distraction from what she really preferred to do, Rita began to accept many aspects of the youth baseball program. Rita started spending time with other mothers of baseball players and formed a supper co-op, a group of six to eight other mothers who take turns providing take-home meals for the other families to eat after games. Rita also learned to let herself occasionally feel sad about not raising a girl, especially around the time of year that would have been her daughter's birthday. Rather than expecting herself to get over it, she created an action step — a ritual to feel compassion for herself and to celebrate all the ways she was fulfilled as a parent. Her vision of being an involved, engaged parent jump-started in a meaningful way.

Through coaching, Rita worked through her resistance and developed acceptance of her children's gender and preference for baseball. Her acceptance did not deny her emotions, but rather gave her a way to honor both herself and her present reality. Acceptance opened the door to appreciation of many elements of her family. Additionally, acceptance energized Rita as she focused her energy on what action steps she could possibly take, rather than on her displeasure in her circumstance. She regained hope.

Rita learned to focus on the health and well-being of her three boys and realized that baseball gave her family structure and incentive to be outside often. Rita loved the outdoors and eventually found a great sense of gratitude that the family had a hobby that involved being outside. Also, Rita grew very fond of the other parents involved in the baseball teams, and she truly cherished these friendships. In accepting rather than resisting the realities of her situation, Rita was able to discover new opportunities for enjoying her family.

Satisfaction comes when the vision and actions line up with the family's needs.

We coach parents to embrace their own personal parenting vision so that at the end of the day they can boldly say, "That was a good day. Let's do it again tomorrow." This level of satisfaction comes when the parent's vision and actions line up with the needs of both the children and the parent.

If you have ever practiced yoga poses, you know the relaxed and energized feeling of alignment when the head, arms, shoulders, hips, legs, and feet are properly aligned in the pose. Alignment provides stability, increases energy flow, and prevents injuries. With any sport, proper form sets up the players to feel more powerful and able to produce the desired results. Similarly, in families, parents can feel successful when their parenting is in alignment: the parent's personality, values, vision, and actions are aligned with the needs of the whole family.

FROM DISTRACTION TO CONNECTION

Randy and Marne were the tech-savvy and career-driven parents of two teens: James, a thirteen-year-old boy and Hayley, a fifteen-year-old girl. The parents' daily choices were not meeting their vision of providing a sense of connection for their children. They were frequently disappointed by the feelings of emptiness in their family life. The parents provided tablets and phones to the children when they turned ten, and both the parents and children spent most of their evenings on their devices.

The parents scheduled their first coaching session in a panic when their daughter did not come home from school one day. After hours of frantic searching, the parents discovered she was with a group of friends the parents didn't know. Even though Hayley was dropped off two hours later unharmed, the parents realized they were largely out of touch with their children's lives. Within a few coaching sessions, the parents accepted the reality that screen technology and media devices were going to be a significant part of their daily life. Additionally, the parents declared a vision that each family member is in touch with each other on every level: school, work, friends, and even with what music each of them liked.

The parents created an action plan that included setting aside time for a ten-to fifteen-minute conversation most evenings and were pleasantly surprised to find out how meaningful the time was for the children as well as for the parents. Sometimes they lingered in conversation much longer. They worked together to make a digital-use plan for the family that left time for connection with each other. Their busy schedules came into alignment with their value to be responsible to one another. Each family member chose to limit their use of one app or game and participate more in conversations. They reported feeling like a family again! The children seemed to feel more secure with clear expectations in place for the family to check in with each other. The parents created a clear plan and were able to prioritize their connection with each other every day.

IT'S YOUR TURN TO TAKE ACTION

It is time for you to answer the questions: *How do you define success?* and *What do you aspire to create in your family?* Parents report feeling more satisfied if their child adopts some of the same values the parent holds dear. A nature-loving parent may be overjoyed when their child wants to spend time outdoors or embarks on a career as a conservationist. Similarly, a parent who regularly attends religious services may feel a sense of immense delight when their child participates enthusiastically in the worship services or chooses to follow in the faith as an adult. Yet, another parent may appreciate their child's sense of individuality, academic interests, or athletic ability that mirrors those of the parent. Are your views of success limited to having a "mini-me" ... a child just like you? Or does it thrill you to see your child develop in ways you could not have imagined?

Look back at your parenting profile from Chapter 1. Keep your values, personality characteristics, and learnings from childhood in mind as you determine which action steps are authentic for you. We encourage parents to experiment with any steps that are in alignment with their vision. Success comes when parents have the mindset to embrace their situation "as is," **and** try on behaviors to grow and change in positive ways.

PILLARS OF PARENTING

Gain clarity and confidence for your own *Real-Time Parenting* vision and action plan by considering these nine pillars of parenting. These nine pillars are parenting behaviors divided into three groups to help you organize your thoughts about making changes in your family.

RELATIONSHIP PILLARS

Attunement: Closely observing and matching parental care to the needs and mood of your child in the moment.

Connection: Demonstrating an interest in your child and growing the parent-child relationship.

Co-parenting: Cultivating a team approach with your parenting partner.

TEACHING PILLARS

Discipline: Teaching right from wrong and following through with rules.

Rituals and Routines: Structuring expectations and daily tasks.

Health and Safety: Protecting your child from harm, promoting physical health, and supporting overall well-being.

SUPPORT PILLARS

Self-care: Providing for your well-being in mind, body, and spirit.

Self-awareness: Noticing your thoughts, feelings, and choices in the moment.

Community: Developing resources for you and your child outside the family.

1. Attunement. Attuning to your baby, child, or teen means that you are aware of how they are doing, and you match your interactions to best respond to the child right where they are. An attuned parent knows the child well and notices their rhythms, preferences, and when they are at their best. The more attuned and responsive the parent is to their child, the more security the child feels in the relationship. Learning and cooperation come out of an attuned relationship.

---

2. Connection. When parents and children connect in a relationship, children feel known, seen, and understood. Connection is a two-way interaction. With a secure connection, parental authority serves to protect and offer comfort to the child. Without a secure connection, parental authority causes power struggles, and feelings of resentment, powerlessness, and even hostility.

---

3. Co-parenting. Teaming up with a co-parent such as your partner, your child's other parent, or other caregiver can provide support and important resources for the parent and child. A healthy co-parenting relationship models important habits and qualities including problem-solving, humor, affection, loyalty, and teamwork.

---

4. Discipline. Discipline means "to teach." With healthy discipline, children learn life skills and good habits to assist on their path to independence. With clear expectations for behavior and predictable follow-through, children learn to behave in ways that best meet their needs.

---

5. Rituals and Routines. Children who experience rituals and routines report feeling secure and supported. These practices put structure in the child's day. They cultivate a sense of belonging. Rituals and routines give the family a sense of flow and predictability, which helps with attachment, emotional regulation, and learning.

6. Health and safety. Health and safety issues are paramount in ensuring your child grows to be physically healthy. Caring for the child's physical needs requires providing a healthy environment and managing risk of injury. Also, focusing on health and safety promotes a sense of well-being and protection, and your child learns good habits to take care of himself.

- -

7. Self-care. Parents who take good care of themselves have a higher level of energy and strength for parenting. Parents who are run down are more likely to act out in ineffective, negative, or hurtful ways. Also, parents are the primary models for children to develop their own sense of value as a human being. Self-care demonstrates self-respect.

- -

8. Self-awareness. With self-awareness, a parent can step back to observe what they are thinking and feeling. This practice helps parents recognize multiple perspectives in a variety of situations. The higher a parent's self-awareness, the more they will be able to stop and notice "survival mode" automatic reactions, and then choose responses that best serve the family vision.

- -

9. Community. Neighborhoods, extended family, recreational facilities, and places of worship are all examples of communities where groups of people gather with common interests. Community gives people extended opportunities to care for one another. Belonging in a community helps meet the overall social and emotional needs of family members to encourage a strong sense of identity and purpose.

- -

Focus on just two or three of these pillars to gain enough clarity to start creating a parenting vision. Your vision is simply what you truly want to create for your family. Once the vision is clear, you can then begin to break through old habits and experiment with an action plan that brings the vision into reality. Parents often describe how the action steps emerge as almost magical. Parental self-doubt is replaced with confident statements set in motion.

Which of the nine pillars capture your attention? Which are the most compelling for you to explore? Please be patient and gentle with yourself as you reflect on your present reality. Choose two or three to focus on today.

THE BRAWLING BROTHERS

 Grace was a mother of two bright boys, ages seven and ten. Both boys demonstrated high achievement on academic tasks and even struggled with getting a bit bored in school when the everyday tasks and their school curriculum did not sufficiently challenge them. The children interacted with peers in their classrooms, yet both reported struggling socially in the cafeteria and at recess. They seemed to have no close friends. The boys got off the bus from school most days elated to see each other; however, their interactions quickly turned into bickering and arguments. Within minutes, they were agitated. They competed in almost every activity and taunted each other mercilessly.

Grace was a quiet, highly intelligent woman in her early forties who valued a peaceful home. She didn't mind having children's toys scattered throughout the house and reported intense devotion to her boys. She radiated with her values of kindness, peacefulness, and inner calm. Yet, she was totally unnerved, felt overwhelming despair, and was flooded with self-doubt when she tried to redirect the boys' arguments. She told of how low she felt when she heard herself yell at the boys to be good to each other. She would often tear up during coaching sessions as she talked about the sadness she felt when her boys couldn't even be at the same dinner table for ten minutes without hurtful arguing.

Through coaching, Grace came to accept her boys for who they truly were

CREATING YOUR PERSONAL VISION

— intelligent children with difficulty managing their emotions. She was drawn to work on the pillars of self-care, attunement, and discipline. Grace aspired to her highest ideals by declaring the vision, "I have a peaceful, enriching, and fun home; my two boys are caring toward each other and excelling in academics. And there is laughter at the dinner table." The coaching process that inspired specific action steps included an inquiry into the nature of sibling rivalry and competition — which may not feel as hostile to the boys as it appeared to Grace. Additionally, Grace discovered many ways she could care for herself, so her boys' interactions were not as overwhelming for her. She reached out to a mom's group that helped her feel less alone in her struggles.

Grace needed a specific plan for addressing the boys' disagreements in order to achieve alignment with her vision. While many friends and even her sympathetic father advised Grace to use consequences for the boys' aggressive behavior, Grace knew it would not feel satisfying to her to use a heavy-handed approach. Grace and her coach worked together to create Grace's vision for her day. Grace realized she needed to structure the day differently so she could interact in a more kind and calm manner, and she timidly began to experiment. She required the boys to go to their separate rooms after school to decompress. She invited them to come to the kitchen one at a time for a snack and some one-on-one time with her. The boys were permitted to interact once they demonstrated the ability to control their energy and emotions, so the fighting was kept to a minimum.

Grace returned to her quieter, calmer self. Within a few months, she and the boys could again be flexible with the after-school routine without returning to the out-of-control fighting. They had created some new habits. Grace acted in alignment with her values by restructuring their routines, and her actions now fit her calm temperament. She now cherishes family time at the dinner table where everyone can share stories and laugh together without fighting.

ASPIRE TO WHERE YOU WANT TO BE

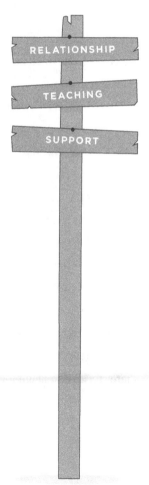

Now that you have prioritized the pillars you want to address, we can look at your aspirations for these areas of parenting. State what you would like to see. For the two or three pillars that most captivate you, create statements that briefly describe, in the present tense, what will be true when you feel fulfilled and satisfied in each area. The examples listed here may jump start your ideas but are not intended to limit your imagination. Avoid "I will," "I want to," "I can," and "I try," and stick with words that indicate you are already doing and experiencing your highest hopes.

Writing your vision statements in the present tense immediately opens up positive feelings and actions toward making them a reality. Keep your statements simple and specific. Feel the energy building.

RELATIONSHIP PILLARS

1) Attunement. Randy: My child and I are in sync. I check in with my children every evening and know their interests in music, friends, and school. Other examples:

- I am aware of my child's daily rhythm for eating, sleeping, and activity.
- I have insight into my child's personality and temperament.
- I respect the differences between my personality and that of my child.
- I am aware of what comforts and motivates my child.

2) Connection. Marne: I feel close to my child and remember she is her own person. I give her space, and she knows that I am here for her.

Other examples:

- I listen to what my child is saying without inserting my opinion.
- I let my child help with age-appropriate decisions.
- I join in games and activities with my child.
- My child and I express affection to each other.

- -

3) Co-parenting. Randy and Marne: We hold each other accountable to be available for our children.

Other examples:

- My co-parent and I are friends as well as co-parents.
- My co-parent and I respect each other and appreciate our different strengths.
- My co-parent and I check in with each other before we make plans.
- My co-parent and I share all relevant information about our child.

- -

TEACHING PILLARS

4) Discipline. Grace: I am reliable and consistent in setting clear expectations for how my boys interact with each other.

Other examples:

- I follow through with what I say I will do.
- I teach life skills to my child.
- I actively support my child's academic progress.
- I adapt my expectations as my child grows.

5) Rituals and Routines (Structure). Grace: Our structured schedule after school helps us all enjoy our time together.

Other examples:

- We have meals together.
- My child consistently takes responsibility for some household chores.
- I communicate family plans to my child.
- There are set expectations in our home for using technology and screens.

---

6) Health and Safety. Marne and Randy: We keep watch over how social media and technology affects the safety of our kids.

Other examples:

- My child has appropriate safety equipment (bed rails, car seat, door locks, etc.).
- My child and I both follow healthy media and technology-use guidelines.
- My child has no access to drugs, alcohol, or weapons.
- My child gets plenty of physical activity.

SUPPORT PILLARS

7) Self-care. Grace: I prioritize my own needs to stay grounded and calm.

Other examples:

- I focus on choices I have rather than feeling sorry for myself.
- I maintain good boundaries on my time and energy.
- I regularly practice a favorite hobby or interest.
- I maintain a growth mindset and learn from my mistakes.

8) Self-awareness. Rita: I give myself freedom to feel all my feelings.
Other examples:

- I keep an open mind.
- I notice my energy level and what energizes me.
- I clear my thoughts through meditation or prayer.
- I notice if I am feeling anxious and am not breathing deeply.

- -

9) Community. Rita: I am part of my sons' activities and engage with the
other families.
Other examples:

- I engage with family, friends, neighbors, and other
  community members regularly.
- I trade babysitting with other families in my neighborhood.
- I engage with the school on parent nights.
- I celebrate events and special occasions with our
  community.

- -

Re-read your vision statements three times. Do they give you a sense of hope? Does your energy level and enthusiasm rise with each reading? We suggest you work with a partner or friend to explore how to state your highest hopes for your family in each of these areas, and notice your confidence surging with each declaration.

Where can you write your vision declarations for the two or three pillars you selected so you will see and read them often? We suggest keeping them fresh by displaying them prominently, or making a vision board, journal, slideshow, or other reminder of the vision declarations that reflect your best self and highest ideals. One parent accepted the reality of a demanding job and aspired to cherish the hands-on parenting by her spouse. She displayed a vision board celebrating all the ways her spouse supports the family while she is away at the office. Another parent made a book of quotes and images displaying her aspirations of high self-esteem and self-worth. A father who managed a large law firm accepted the reality he had a strong, domineering personality. He aspired to have an atmosphere of mutual problem-solving in his home with his two teenage sons. He wrote the words, "we are a team" on post-it notes and left them in his car, his bathroom, and on the coffee pot. He even invited his children to help him remember to listen to their ideas before important decisions were made.

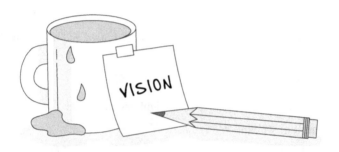

Acceptance and aspiration are a continuous loop for reflection in the visioning process. Your vision will change over time as your children grow, and as you learn and progress in your parenting journey. Each step along the way will emerge and evolve as you learn. Congratulations on your progress creating the vision statements that are most meaningful to you.

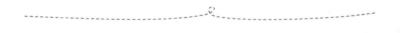

Vision without action is merely a dream. Action without vision just passes the time. Vision with action can change the world.
Joel A. Barker

THE MAGIC OF THE PARENT-CHILD RELATIONSHIP

In this chapter, we invite you to explore:

- The importance of the parent-child relationship
- Effective tools to encourage open communication
- The benefits of intentional listening

The parent-child relationship is truly the heart and soul of parenting. The quality of the relationship is defined by the level of connection. The relationship you have with your child can play a pivotal role in your child's development. A strong parent-child relationship increases the impact of everything you would like to teach your children **and** increases the joy you can experience as a parent. Therein lies the magic. As you begin to integrate your parenting vision into real-time action, remember that it is never too late to improve your connection with your child.

From the first moment we discover we are expecting a child, we begin to envision our relationship with our child. Many parents begin to bond before the baby is born, singing or reading to their unborn child. We imagine the bond we will experience on our parenting journey from the first cry, to the first step, to first grade, to the first school dance, and perhaps even to the first day of college. And we now know that our dreams and desires are more than simply yearnings, they are supported by science.

Research from neuroscientists confirms that the human brain is hard wired for social interaction. Our children have a biological need for connection. In addition, our brains have amazing neuroplasticity and can reorganize and create new neural connections throughout life. So, our opportunities to improve our relationships with our children are truly endless.

We have learned from many experts over the decades, from Alfred Adler to Maria Montessori to Brené Brown, that a key element of human development is the sense of belonging. This is formed through the parent-child relationship. The connection that began when you first laid eyes on your child activated her sense of belonging. And through ordinary moments, day in and day out, you continue to support your child's need to belong as an integral part of the family and community.

Our children also have a social and emotional need for connection. They need skills to navigate the challenges of our culture now as much as ever. These skills include: understanding and regulating one's thoughts and feelings; having awareness and compassion for others and effectively cooperating with others; making responsible decisions and effectively solving problems; and communicating and interacting positively with others. Nearly every professional field including education, medicine, business, and technology has a new focus on these skills.

A child's early relationship with family members helps set the stage for social skills development. Simple play teaches children about taking turns and interacting with others. Constructive family interactions promote understanding of different perspectives and offer practice with problem-solving in order to meet significant needs. Emotional skills are developed when family members share their feelings of love and joy or hurt and anger. Children develop an awareness of these emotions and slowly learn to regulate them. The parent-child relationship is the foundation for the development of these increasingly important social and emotional skills. As the Center on the Developing Child at Harvard University emphasizes, "Relationships also help build resilience across childhood and into adulthood. The single most common factor for children and teens who develop the capacity to overcome serious hardship is having at least one stable and committed relationship with a supportive parent, caregiver, or other adult."

The relationship you develop helps your children in a variety of ways and can show up in real-time moments. Your preschooler may return to you repeatedly as you're sitting on the bench at the park. Your eight-year-old may need your undivided attention when you return home from work at the end of the day. Your twelve-year-old may need extra time to talk through an issue at bedtime. Your teenager may pick a fight with you over a mundane topic in order to experience a bond with you (as crazy as that seems!). Even your college student may send frequent text messages during her first semester away.

> The parent-child relationship is the vehicle for guiding children through the inevitable ups and downs of life.

Every child is unique, and each parent-child relationship is unique. Parents who continually nurture this magical bond with their children will have greater impact on the connection with their child. Look back at Chapter 3 and see where you rated yourself on the connection pillar. Do you feel present and responsive to your child? Does your connection help your child feel seen and heard? Would it help to be more intentional as you nurture your connection?

TUNING IN TO EVERYDAY MOMENTS

When we bring awareness to our everyday moments, when we slow down and tune in to the child in front of us, we enhance our connection. Slowing down might mean pausing in the moment and visually taking in what is happening right in front of us. It might mean pausing our thoughts and taking a break from our mental to-do list. It might mean pausing our actions and simply experiencing the moment, as A. A. Milne reminds us:

"Pooh!" he whispered.

"Yes, Piglet?"

"Nothing," said Piglet, taking Pooh's paw. "I just wanted to be sure of you."

Creating awareness and being present to our children is not an easy task. Presence takes practice, yet it is accessible to all of us. Jon Kabat-Zinn refers to this presence as mindfulness, "Mindfulness means paying attention in a particular way: on purpose, in the present moment, and non-judgmentally." Kabat-Zinn invites us to be aware of the present moment. It can be difficult to be solely focused on what is right in front of us without lamenting about the past or fretting about the future. Yet, when we intentionally practice slowing down and tuning in, we practice mindfulness and we gain awareness.

Young children often experience the present moment with greater ease. A five-year-old walking to school sees a ladybug. She immediately crouches down to watch it crawl. She tries to pick it up. She does not think about yesterday, when she was late and the last one to walk into her kindergarten class. She is not worried about what will happen if she dawdles too long today. She is simply in the moment, observing the ladybug.

When parents take advantage of these ordinary moments and follow their child's lead, they help build connection. It is easy to get distracted and miss the small moments. Can you create space in your day to notice these moments? This may mean briefly putting your to-do list on hold or putting your phone away to be present for your child.

Practice tuning in to ordinary micro-moments. Simply observe your child without evaluating the interaction, without evaluating your child, without evaluating yourself. If your child stops to look at a ladybug, you can simply pause in silence and be present to her experience. You might comment, "What an interesting ladybug." If the looming school bell is calling you to move on, you might say, "How about we take a picture of the ladybug so that you can make it to school on time." Taking thirty seconds to connect in the moment helps children feel seen and heard.

Prioritizing connection in real time looks different for each of us. A parent who values productivity may find it difficult to stop and look at ladybugs. This parent may focus on the relationship while folding laundry or doing dishes with her child. Another parent who values creativity may bond while tinkering with a motorbike in the garage. Take advantage of the possibilities as they show up in real time moments.

Look for emotional connection during the simple moments of the day. When you make your child breakfast in the morning, take a moment to appreciate the child in front of you without worrying about getting out the door. When you pick your child up at the end of the day, look in her eyes and ask about her day without thinking about emails or the dinner menu. When driving your child to practice, eliminate distractions by turning off the radio and tuning in to the brief opportunity to talk about the day.

We often talk about doing and have endless to-do lists written on paper, typed in devices, or rumbling through in our heads. But what does it look like when we are just being? It is helpful to remember that we are human beings, not human doings. When do you have a chance to just be?

MOMENTS OF MINDFULNESS MAKE ALL THE DIFFERENCE

Tara felt frustrated listening to her son, Charlie, whine and complain about doing his homework. She was reminded of her own challenges and failures as a student. Tara began to experiment by focusing on the present moment with Charlie and brought her full attention to conversations with him. As Tara focused on the here-and-now, she found that her fears about past problems and anxiety about future challenges diminished. She began to honor Charlie's third-grade journey without tying it to her past. Tara learned to catch herself when anxious thoughts crept in and continually brought her focus back to the present moment.

Peter wanted to deepen his connection with his twelve-year-old son, Viktor. He planned to focus on their connection while driving together to soccer practice. Instead of peppering his son with questions about the next big game, Peter invited Viktor to tune in to his favorite radio station. The two then chatted about the music or simply listened together in silence. Peter began to appreciate these ordinary moments of connection with more intention and felt a new level of closeness with his son.

Louisa struggled to connect with her teenage son who spent much of his free time gaming. She decided to approach the situation through a lens of connection. Louisa took a few moments to watch her son play and then quietly asked questions about the game. She worked to utilize his interest in gaming as a vehicle for connection.

ENHANCING CONNECTION

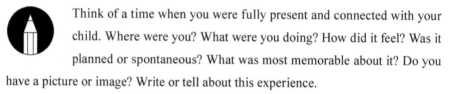

Think of a time when you were fully present and connected with your child. Where were you? What were you doing? How did it feel? Was it planned or spontaneous? What was most memorable about it? Do you have a picture or image? Write or tell about this experience.

Can you relive the details in this present moment? Can you create the same feeling and connection today? How can you be present in an ordinary moment today?

Consider the rhythm of your day. Can you connect with your kids while folding laundry? Cutting potatoes? Walking the dog? Going to the grocery store? Are there ways to connect nonverbally by holding hands or giving backrubs? How do you naturally tune in and connect with each of your children? What might you do differently to enhance your connection?

USING COMMUNICATION TO ENHANCE RELATIONSHIPS

The way we communicate with our children can have an enormous impact on our relationship with them. What we say and how we say it can either enhance or detract from our connection. Learning to communicate effectively can help children feel seen, heard, and understood, which cultivates a stronger parent-child bond.

Dan Siegel refers to communication as "a reciprocal give-and-take of signals." He describes it as communicating so "that the signals sent by the child are directly perceived, understood, and responded to by the parent in a dance of communication that involves mutual collaboration ... This contingent communication enables a vitalizing sense of connection that may be at the heart of nurturing relationships across the life span."

When your baby first began to smile and you were focused on this wondrous new stage, you likely used this back and forth communication. You were present and aware that your child was communicating with you and you eagerly responded with words and smiles that kept the dance of communication going.

You likely paid great attention to your baby's nonverbal cues. A grimace might indicate a wet diaper, droopy eyes signal bedtime, and clenched fists means discomfort of some sort. Nonverbal communication continues throughout the parent-child relationship. We see the excitement on our third-grader's face when she opens a birthday party invitation; our middle-schooler begins to shrug his shoulders rather than use words; and our teenage daughter becomes proficient at using the eye-roll. As parents we might sigh or throw up our hands in frustration. Other moments, we beam with love and pride.

How do we achieve responsive communication as parents? How do we truly listen with an open mind and respond in an effective way? So many parents are juggling different thoughts and actions when they are interacting with their children. They have one eye on their phone and are thinking about what to make for dinner, all while trying to respond to their child who has asked them a question. They often say, "Just one minute," when they really mean, "It might be fifteen minutes before I can focus on what you are saying or doing." It can be difficult to **always** be attuned to your child. When do you notice being able to pay close attention rather than being distracted?

We can transform our relationships in meaningful ways when we bring awareness to how and when we listen.

Shefali Tsabary points out that parents sometimes mistake being busy with their children as having a present connection, "Though we may be present for their material, physical, and even intellectual needs, this doesn't mean we are present for their emotional and spiritual needs ... if we wish to connect with our children of any age group, we need to find a way to match *their* emotional energy ... which allows them to become receptive." Matching children's emotional energy requires noticing their facial expressions and words and adjusting our behavior to meet children where they are.

Bill's teenage daughters were not ready for their father's new girlfriend to spend the weekend with them in the family home. They were shocked when their father exuberantly declared a weekend full of activities for the four of them. The girls would have preferred their father tuned in to their needs. They would have appreciated for him to ask what would help them feel comfortable for including his girlfriend in the weekend.

THE FLIP SIDE OF CONNECTION

Parents may mistakenly believe they are connecting with their children when they are overly involved. As we discussed in Chapter 1, over involvement is often called "helicopter parenting," hovering over children either physically or emotionally. When parents mistake connection and communication with hovering, they swoop in to correct or fix, denying their children an opportunity to understand themselves and wrestle with their own issues. Other parents are seen as "snowplow parents," paving the way for their children so there are no obstacles or surprises that might challenge the child. This unknowingly conveys the message the child is too fragile to solve problems or overcome challenges.

We encourage parents to be aware of their level of involvement and consider how it aligns with their child's age and developmental stage. Letting go of involvement doesn't need to be done at the expense of connection with your child. You can remain supportive and present without overtaking aspects of your child's life. Honor your children's ability to take responsibility for their unique challenges and accomplishments.

REAL-TIME OPPORTUNITIES TO CONNECT

Briana came to coaching looking for less stress and more enjoyment with her two children, Malik and Tia. As a single mom, Briana felt that her days were a jumble of full-time work, household management, and parental duties. Much of her family time was spent nagging or rushing Malik and Tia, with little opportunity to simply enjoy them. Briana yearned to feel confident about completing work and home tasks and to find greater joy in her interactions with Malik and Tia.

Briana worked with her coach to take a closer look at her daily interactions. She realized that when it came to chores, Briana either yelled at the kids when chores weren't done properly or shooed them away so she could complete them herself. Briana decided on a new approach. She invited Malik and Tia to help her prepare dinner. At age five, Tia was capable of washing vegetables and setting the table. Malik, age fourteen, cut vegetables or cooked on the stove. Both kids helped clean up once dinner was done. Briana also got the children involved in laundry. When the clothes came out of the dryer, Malik folded shirts and pants, Tia sorted socks, and Briana organized the piles of clothes. Briana continued to look for age-appropriate opportunities for her children to pitch in with household chores. Joining together to complete the tasks helped conquer the chore list **and** improved family connections.

ROADBLOCKS TO COMMUNICATION AND CONNECTION

Parents often inadvertently create barriers when they communicate with their children. Thomas Gordon, a psychologist widely recognized for his models of effective communication, calls these barriers, "Communication Roadblocks." These are typical responses that tend to stop communication and deny feelings. They are often the parent's attempt to change the way their child thinks, feels, or acts. Gordon's "Communication Roadblocks" are listed here with examples to illustrate how they might sound.

Criticizing, Judging, Blaming

Oh no — why do you always make such a mess?

What have you done now to upset your sister?

If you had studied more this would not have happened.

Threatening, Warning

If you can't listen to me, we will have to leave.

Don't use that tone with me, or else ...

You better start working harder if you want to go to college!

Name Calling, Ridiculing

You sound like a baby and not like a big boy.

Why are you always so afraid to try something new?

This happens because you are so lazy!

Lecturing, Teaching

If you hadn't eaten so many cookies, you wouldn't feel sick.

You just need to stop that so that your friends will like you.

You better go talk to your teacher and ask her to give you another chance.

Ordering, Directing, Demanding

Stop whining!

You need to change your attitude.

Clean up this room right now!

Moralizing, Preaching

You have got to learn to keep your hands to yourself.

You weren't raised to act this way.

You don't realize how important it is to work hard.

Reassuring, Sympathizing

I know you didn't mean to hurt him.

Don't worry, it's going to be fine.

You will look back at this and laugh someday.

Diverting, Withdrawing, Distracting

How about we play this instead?

Did you hear what happened to your brother today?

You wouldn't have wanted to be on that team anyway. Let's go get pizza.

Questioning, Probing, Interrogating

Why can't you behave?

Where did you learn that?

Why would you do that? What were you thinking?

Praising, Buttering Up

You are such a good boy!

Don't worry, you are smart enough to figure it out.

Well, I think you look fantastic.

Advising, Giving Solutions

This is the best way to do it.

You need to work harder, then you'll make the team.

I think you need to tell your teacher before you do anything else.

Interpreting, Analyzing

I think you are just too tired to be nice.

You don't really believe that, you're just confused.

It seems as if you don't really want it, otherwise you would make a different choice.

Parents often mean well when they respond to their children yet may be sending messages they didn't intend to send. Consider three-year-old Achta adjusting to a new baby in her family. Achta stomps her feet and says, "I hate the baby! I wish he could go back to the hospital!" Many well-meaning parents would naturally respond saying, "You don't hate your baby brother. We love everyone in our family."

A child who is told how she feels ("You don't hate your baby brother! You love everyone") may feel guilt or shame or confusion. She may respond to the implication of how she ought to feel by defending her stance. The conversation with Achta might sound like this:

Mom: *You don't hate your baby brother. We love everyone in our family.*

Achta: *Yes I do hate him! I wish he wasn't here!*

Mom: *We don't say 'hate' in this family.*

Achta: (beginning to cry and yell): *Hate. Hate. Hate!*

Mom: *You need to have a time-out if you are going to yell those words.*

What is Achta really feeling and experiencing regarding the new baby in the family? What is the need behind her words and behavior? Did her mother's response address that feeling? Or did she try to change the feelings of their three-year-old? Which roadblocks did Mom use?

Other times, our roadblocks can sound more encouraging, but still interfere with connection. Consider this scenario when ten-year-old Becca comes home from school in tears.

Becca: *Emily isn't my friend anymore!*

Dad: *What happened between you and Emily?*

Becca: *She invited Carly and Madison to her party and said I wasn't invited.*

Dad: *Did you do something to upset her?*

Becca: *She got mad at me because I didn't want her to be team captain when we played soccer at recess today.*

Dad: *Well why don't you tell her you are sorry tomorrow. And ask her to be team captain at recess, too. She'll forget all about being mad at you.*

In this scenario, do you think Becca feels understood? Was her true need met? Do you think Becca felt a greater connection to her father? Which roadblocks did Becca's dad use?

Parents typically do not intend these unwanted thoughts or feelings to develop in their children, yet initial parental reactions, or roadblocks, create them. Children often feel threatened, demoralized, or fearful. Some responses seem to say the child is incapable or inferior, that they cannot be counted on to address their own issue and come up with their own solution. Other responses may evoke anger or defensiveness in children.

Often our messages inadvertently negate our child's need. The communication Mom used with Achta might leave Achta feeling misunderstood as well as insignificant. Perhaps her unmet need was one of acceptance during the transition time of a new baby. Becca's dad may have sent a message that she is incapable of solving her own problems right when she needs to feel accepted by others.

When our knee-jerk reaction sounds like blaming, threatening, ordering, lecturing, fixing, or any of the other roadblocks, we unintentionally inhibit communication, negate feelings, and dismiss needs. We have worked with many parents who have improved their interactions with their children simply by becoming more aware of their use of roadblocks. Rather than swooping in with criticism, demands, lectures, or even praise, they take the real-time step to avoid roadblocks. By doing this, they alter the interaction with their child. They have learned to be present in real time, to slow down, tune in, and mindfully avoid roadblocking their communications.

NOTICE ROADBLOCKS

 Do you hear people using roadblocks during an ordinary day? Do you hear them at your workplace? At the grocery story? Between you and your parenting partner or child? On TV shows? Keep notes for one week of the roadblocks you notice. Review your notes and consider how the roadblocks affect communication. It is helpful to first notice roadblocks in your daily communication. The next step is to consider effective practices to enhance connection.

TEN TOOLS FOR YOUR PARENTING TOOLKIT

 Hold your vision in one hand and a toolkit filled with best practices for authoritative parenting in the other. Listed below are effective practices, or tools, that encourage a directive and responsive approach. These are skills that when combined with your vision help to create your personal action plan.

We explore these tools in subsequent chapters and invite you to practice them in real time:

1. Listen with intention
2. Provide encouragement
3. Use descriptive language
4. Offer choices
5. Give clear and firm directions
6. Set up the physical space to fit your goals
7. Establish effective routines
8. Set rules and follow through with them

9. Use appropriate consequences

10. Solve problems together

LISTEN WITH INTENTION

Our first tool helps parents respond to their children in more effective, helpful ways. We encourage parents to recognize roadblocks and replace them with a listening response. Intentional listening means listening for the feelings behind your child's words or behaviors and accepting them without judgment. Other terms used to describe this tool are active listening, empathetic listening, validating feelings, and reflective listening.

When we intentionally listen, we respect our child's right to have feelings. We may not always understand or appreciate the feelings, yet when we respectfully accept them, we validate our child's feelings and experiences. We help our children feel truly heard and understood. When we offer space with listening, we offer a chance for an unmet need to surface. When we pause and connect before we redirect, we strengthen our connection and improve our relationships.

> One of the most impactful tools to connect with children is intentional listening.

We connect in a powerful way when our children feel understood, when their feelings and experiences are validated. Take the example of eight-year-old Ellie, whose family is preparing to move. Ellie states, "I don't want to move to the new house!" A natural reaction to Ellie might be to reassure her and redirect the conversation to more positive aspects of the move. "You are going to love your new bedroom! And we will have a big yard for playing!" Yet, when we first validate the uneasy feeling, and let Ellie truly experience it, we are giving her an opportunity to accept, understand, and process her feelings. We can repeat what she says so that she feels we get it, "You don't want to move." We can name the feeling we suspect, "You are sad to leave this bedroom." We can accept the feeling with silence or a simple response, "Hmmm ...". We can validate thoughts and feelings by imagining what she would prefer, "You wish we could live in this house forever." Or we can honor her feelings by offering to write down what she would prefer, "Let's write down what you feel is important about this bedroom." When we lead with listening, and we acknowledge and accept feelings, we give our children space to process them. They are then more willing to hear and accept our reassurances or redirection to the positive aspects of the move.

Listening is a key concept in *The Art of Positive Parenting* by Mickey Tobin. She teaches six primary ways to listen to feelings:

- Mirror back what you have heard.
- Pause without responding, be silent.
- Validate the feeling, name it for the child.
- Use a simple, one-word response (Hmm … Wow … Really …).
- Use imagination (You wish …).
- Write the feeling down.

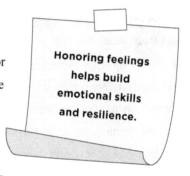

Honoring feelings helps build emotional skills and resilience.

Marc Brackett, Director of the Yale Center for Emotional Intelligence, dives into the importance of understanding and navigating emotions in his compelling book, *Permission to Feel*. He highlights five skills necessary to understand and manage emotions — RULER skills — Recognizing, Understanding, Labeling, Expressing, and Regulating emotions. Intentional listening helps children with this process. We help our children recognize and begin to understand the emotion. And when we use words to label the feeling, we begin to help kids express and regulate their emotions. Brackett states, "Labeling emotions accurately increases self-awareness and helps us to communicate emotions effectively, reducing misunderstanding in social interactions." This helps our children understand themselves **and** improves our connection with them.

Learning to recognize and accept feelings is like many aspects of parenting — we need to start with ourselves. It is difficult to notice and name our children's emotions if we ignore or numb our own. Brackett states, "You teach your children to express their emotions by skillfully expressing yours. This is why we adults need to be open to learning and practicing strategies in our own emotional lives before we can support our kids." When parents honor and understand their own emotions, they are better prepared to positively address those of their children.

When adults build and model emotion skills, they not only help themselves and their children, but they also help the broader community. When we truly listen with intention, we can hear the words and experiences of others. This allows a deeper appreciation and understanding of others, especially those who are different from us. Brackett reminds us, "Emotion skills are a bulwark against the epidemic of anger, bullying, disengagement, anxiety, and dread in the country, especially among young people."

Intentional listening is a powerful tool to help you communicate and connect with your child. Tsabary emphasizes the need for listening as we connect with our children in the present moment. She states, "Meeting our children's need for connection requires a particular set of skills. It means we listen to our children, truly hearing what they are saying without feeling we have to fix, correct, or lecture." When our goal is to listen and to be truly present to our children's experience without bringing in our agenda, we not only enhance the relationship, we also honor our children's experiences. If those experiences include struggles, we honor their ability to sit in their struggles, rather than rushing in to rescue them or fix things for them.

Listening is not about being soft or being unresponsive, it's about being strong enough to let go and trust your child to experience and manage the situation. By allowing our children to struggle, we empower them to know their own strength. We give them the message that they can do this, we don't have to do it for them.

TRICKY TRICK-OR-TREAT

 It was Halloween and the first year Brooke's ten-year-old, Caden, was going to trick-or-treat after school with his buddies without parents tagging along. He burst through the front door at 3:05, announcing he would **not** be trick-or-treating. Brooke's automatic response would have been, "What do you mean you're not going trick-or-treating? I thought you were going with Jack. Did you and Jack have a problem at school today?" (Each response a roadblock — Questioning, Probing, Interpreting).

Brooke has a sensitive, emotional personality style so it was painful to see Caden struggling with his trick-or-treat plans. She typically would rush in to soothe the situation for Caden but had recently learned about Thomas Gordon's "Communication Roadblocks" through coaching, so she practiced intentional listening instead.

"Hmmm … You've changed your plan about trick-or-treating."

"There is no one to go with," Caden stated, on the verge of tears.

Brooke's practice was being put to the test. It would be so natural to say, "I told you three days ago to call Jack and make a plan." (Preaching) Or, "That's okay. I would love to trick-or-treat with you!" (Buttering up, Giving solutions) Brooke remembered how Caden used to retreat and slam the door when she gave advice in the past. Instead, she gently touched him on the arm and simply said, "There are no friends to go trick-or treating … bummer." Caden responded, "Jack said he is going with Ben in his neighborhood."

Caden was actually talking. Brooke continued with listening responses. Rather than suggesting the next logical course of action, that he call another friend (Giving solutions), she empathized with him, "That's disappointing. You wanted to trick-or-treat with Jack, but he is going with Ben." Then to her utter surprise, Caden came up with his own solution. "Maybe Luke will want to go with me. I think I'll call him."

We can just imagine Caden's response if Brooke had suggested he call Luke. By replacing typical roadblocks with intentional listening, Caden was able to work through his disappointment and solve his own problem. He donned his superman costume and soon Luke, the Ninja warrior, appeared at the door. Off they went to fill their pillowcases with candy. Instead of micromanaging the situation, Brooke allowed Caden to wrestle with his feelings and his experience. They both learned that he was able to solve his own issue.

We invite you to recognize the innate need for connection in all of us. Then show up each day by tuning in and practicing presence and awareness. Notice your use of roadblocks and replace them with intentional listening. See how tuning into connection and communication supports your vision. As you take these *Real-Time Parenting* steps, you offer a deep connection in the joyful moments and the challenging ones.

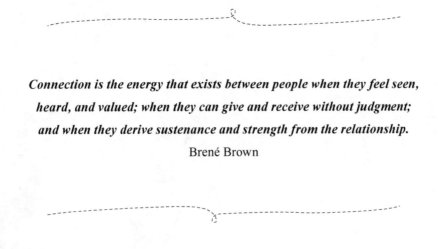

Connection is the energy that exists between people when they feel seen, heard, and valued; when they can give and receive without judgment; and when they derive sustenance and strength from the relationship.
Brené Brown

INFLUENCING YOUR CHILD'S BEHAVIOR

In this chapter we invite you to:

- Gain insight about your children's behaviors
- Learn communication strategies to improve interactions
- Set up your daily routine to support your vision

In our work with parents, the first topic they want to discuss often deals with behavior. They ask: How can I get my children to stop fighting with one another? What should I do when she won't eat her dinner, or he forgets to wear his bike helmet, or she uses bad language, or he doesn't do his homework? The list goes on and on. Behavior is a real-time issue on the minds of many parents. And yet, we did not place this topic first. We purposely placed this topic in Chapter 5 because if there is one thing we have learned over the decades, it is that parents can positively influence behavior once they understand themselves, know their children, clarify their desires, and focus on a connected relationship. When we attend to these foundational concepts first, we have fewer behavior challenges to address.

How our children behave — their response to situations, their reaction to our guidance, their actions and attitudes — impacts every interaction we have with them. When our children behave as we would like them to, interactions feel positive. When our children behave in ways that are upsetting or disappointing, we often feel angry, annoyed, or confused. We feel the urge to control the situation; we feel the need to control our children. Yet, the truth is we cannot control another human being. Every person is ultimately in control of their own actions.

Intentional language and effective routines in a supportive environment help influence children's behavior.

A key concept we explain to parents is that outward behaviors reflect the child's inner world. Children often behave the way they feel. Behaviors are often messages that reflect met or unmet needs. When we look under the surface of our child's behavior with curiosity and compassion, we discover what our child may be feeling. In our work with parents we discover the root causes of a child's behavior. With this understanding, the parent explores new responses with better results.

SAD

CONFUSED

SCARED

FRUSTRATED

ANGRY

PAUSE AND LOOK BENEATH THE SURFACE

We can consider behavior as an iceberg. Words and actions are above the surface, while causes and motivation lie beneath the surface. To gain an understanding of what is really going on with our child — what he is trying to communicate through his behavior — we need to suspend judgment and investigate. We find the teachings of Marshall Rosenberg, the founder of the Center for Nonviolent Communication (NVC), helpful in understanding the depths of human behavior. Rosenberg's theory is that all human interactions are an attempt to meet a need, and all humans share basic core needs. Understanding the core needs of self and others helps us find common ground in our relationships. Rosenberg tested his compassionate communication approach in many different cultural and high conflict situations and his theory stood up to the claim of universal applicability. When we gain clarity of what our child needs, we are better able to address the behavior effectively. When we take the time to understand another person's true needs, we gain compassion, reduce conflict, and strengthen relationships.

Imagine your four-year-old is having a particularly difficult morning. He is extra clingy to you as you dress for work. He bursts into tears when he can't open his yogurt. He walks past his baby sister and he squeezes her so hard she begins to cry. Rather than solely focusing on the undesirable behavior, consider the underlying message behind the behavior. The baby was sick all weekend and needed more of your attention. Your four-year-old is looking for extra attention and reassurance this morning. He needs to be reminded that he is as important as his baby sister. When we pause and consider the possible need behind the behavior, we are better prepared to address it.

Let's look at some additional examples.

Your child repeatedly leaves the table during family dinner despite several requests to stay in his seat. Is your child feeling antsy — does he need to move his body? Is he feeling unnoticed — does he need attention?

Your two children are working on a puzzle. One sits quietly working on the puzzle with you while the other walks up and throws pieces on the floor. Is your child feeling unskilled at the puzzle and in need of reassurance? Is he feeling disconnected and in need of attention?

Your teenager clearly knows the family rules for using the internet and phone, yet she repeatedly disregards them. Does she need more consideration and input into creating the rules? More guidance? More freedom?

How do you effectively guide your children's behavior **and** meet their needs? Rather than engaging in a power struggle, notice your expectations and whether or not they are realistic. Put yourself in your child's shoes and consider what is going on in real time.

Some parents come to coaching exasperated, describing their child's behavior as defiant or impossible. The work of Ross Greene, child psychologist and author, provides powerful insights for understanding and managing challenging behaviors. Greene makes an impactful yet simple point, "Children do well when they can." This message helps parents remember their child is not **choosing** to be difficult. The child may still be learning ways to be flexible and to tolerate frustration. Be curious and consider how your child's temperament and developmental stage affect their behavior. As you tune in to what is going on with your child, you can begin to practice tools to boost cooperation and teach self-regulation.

PROVIDE ENCOURAGEMENT

A key tool to influence behaviors and attitudes is encouragement. We offer encouragement by bringing our attention and energy to desirable behaviors and attitudes we appreciate. Encouragement is noticing and reinforcing what is working. And, as Jane Nelsen states in her book *Positive Discipline*, "Encouragement is teaching children the life skills and social responsibility they need to be successful in life and relationships."

When we encourage our children, we boost their confidence and instill in them a desire to explore and grow.

Parents naturally provide encouragement at times. Think about when your child took her first steps. Once you saw her attempt this exciting milestone you no doubt perched eagerly near her, eyes fixed on her every move, clapping and exclaiming your joy and amazement as she put one foot in front of the other. Your full attention and energy were fixated on those little feet. Can you bring that attention and energy to everyday moments? It may feel overboard to respond to a clean bedroom, a completed school project, or an honored curfew with clapping or shouts of joy. If we want to encourage behaviors we are hoping to develop in our children, we need to treat these **expected** behaviors with attention and appreciation.

Parents tell us that mornings can be a particularly difficult time. We wake our children up with a smile and are greeted with frowns and groans. We ask our kids to get dressed and come to breakfast, and they start wrestling with one another; they can't find the pants they want to wear; and they want to have cereal instead of the eggs we have prepared. We need them to be responsible, and they need to connect in disruptive ways. We repeatedly ask them to stop wrestling, lecture them about setting their clothes out the night before, and convince them of the healthy merits of eggs. They leave for school feeling incompetent and dejected. We feel frustrated and guilty. Is there a better way?

USE ENCOURAGEMENT TO INFLUENCE BEHAVIOR

Jennifer and her family were experiencing chaos and frustration with their morning routine. Ten-year-old twin boys, Trevor and Jake, and seven-year-old daughter Lilly, had difficulty getting dressed on their own, eating breakfast in a timely manner, and getting out the door to catch the school bus. The kids would dawdle, shift their attention to other activities, and often miss the bus. Who knew getting shoes on could cause a major meltdown? Jennifer constantly repeated directions to the point of yelling and berating the kids. She felt annoyed and angry most mornings.

Through coaching, Jennifer realized how much she valued responsibility and order. Jennifer clarified her vision: she yearned for a predictable morning routine. As she focused on the morning interactions, she noticed that she often ignored expected behaviors yet paid attention to annoying behaviors. When the twins got up on time and started to get dressed, Jennifer headed downstairs without interfering, yet when they started wrestling with one another, she would enter their room and repeatedly say, "Stop messing around and get dressed!" When her daughter was eating breakfast as expected, Jennifer would take a moment to check her email. When Lilly would dawdle, Jennifer would remind her, "Eat your breakfast so that you don't miss the bus today!" Jennifer also realized how often she was distracted by her cell phone. She would check her texts, emails, and the weather while shrieking the fifth request to come to breakfast.

Working with her coach, Jennifer planned to focus on the behaviors she wanted to reinforce in order to create an effective morning routine. She focused her attention on behaviors she expected her kids to do. She began to notice the parts of the morning routine that were going well and used descriptive language to bring her attention to these positive behaviors: "Trevor, you got up and used the bathroom right when your alarm went off. Lilly, you are enjoying your waffles today!" This encouraged the kids to focus on their morning tasks. Jennifer shifted her attention to the tasks she wanted the kids to do — the "do behaviors," rather than reprimanding the "don't behaviors." Instead of saying, "Boys — stop wrestling or you will be late for school," she would state, "When you have your shoes on, you will be able to get to the bus stop on time."

Jennifer also removed her phone from the morning chaos. She began a new habit of checking texts before waking the kids and reading emails after they were out the door. The family decided to mount a thermometer outside the kitchen window, so they could check the temperature without using a cell phone. Jennifer and her kids experienced a new morning routine with the three kids taking responsibility and Jennifer feeling peaceful.

When we use encouragement to influence behaviors, we create a positive environment which typically results in more desirable, respectful interactions with our children. We treat our children with respect and set the stage to receive respect. We center our attention and communication on desired behaviors, which helps us have greater energy and optimism for the job of parenting.

TOO MUCH PRAISE?

There is a lot of discussion and research about the merits of praise. However, praise may cause some children to become pleasers and approval junkies and other children to feel rebellious or anxious because they don't want to, or simply can't, live up to the expectations of others. We often praise our children with comments such as:

Good job!
You are awesome!
You are so smart!
You are excellent at math!

Yet when children continually receive this type of generic praise, it becomes habitual to look outward for affirmation. Rather than building a strong inner sense of self, we inadvertently nudge our kids to look to others to help build their sense of self. Nelson states, "The long-term effect of praise invites dependence on others." Instead of praise that evaluates with a stamp of generic approval, Nelsen invites us to use encouragement — statements that are respectful and inspire self-evaluation and self-confidence.

When your child shows you a picture she has made, instead of lavishing praise, "Wow that is a beautiful picture! You are a great artist!" practice using descriptive language, "I see a rainbow and a blue pond with three colorful fish! You used so many colors in your picture!"

USE DESCRIPTIVE LANGUAGE

 Stanford psychologist, Carol Dweck, supports the merits of descriptive language in her groundbreaking work regarding motivation and mindset. Dweck believes parents can help their children develop a "growth mindset" — a belief that abilities can be developed. This belief encourages motivation and builds resilience. In her book, *Mindset*, Dweck states, "The passion for stretching yourself and sticking to it, even (or especially) when it's not going well, is the hallmark of the growth mindset. This is the mindset that allows people to thrive during some of the most challenging times in their lives." Dweck teaches us that if we focus on effort and the learning process, rather than talent or outcome, challenges can become an opportunity to learn from mistakes and try new strategies.

Parents mean well when they say, "Excellent job picking up your room. You are amazing." We have complimented our child for work well done, yet we are putting our stamp of approval on the job and the child. Instead, we can simply say, "The bed is made. The clothes are in the hamper. And all the books are on the shelf. That is what I call a clean room!" By describing what we see, we allow the child to bring the experience inward. He may say to himself, "Yep — I did an awesome job," or "I am good at cleaning up my room." Rather than looking to others for approval and recognition, he looks inward and feels appreciation for himself. Our awareness and appreciation of the clean room helps develop values in our children, even if they value messy rooms as teenagers!

Descriptive language can be useful in a variety of interactions. You can use it to express your concern or frustration in a way that respects your child and enhances the relationship. When you address a challenging situation in a matter-of-fact way, you avoid messages that sound like emotional, judgmental lectures.

> Hearing language that describes behavior helps children develop their sense of self and internal compass.

Teenagers love to borrow their parents' car, yet often repay the favor by leaving the car in disarray. Our frustration may sound like this: "You are so inconsiderate. I am never letting you use my car again!" We are angry and our anger turns into shaming, labeling, and threatening. We can use descriptive language to share frustration and anger while honoring our connection and respecting our child, "When you drove the car the other night you left fast food bags and empty water bottles on the floor. It is very frustrating to lend a clean car and get a dirty one returned."

Descriptive language helps bring your attention to behaviors and attitudes in a nonjudgmental way. It is a tool to connect with the child in front of you, in real-time moments, and shine a light of awareness on what you see without analyzing, evaluating, or correcting. It is simple, yet not easy to do. When we practice using descriptive language, we note what is working, what is going well. We are better able to encourage our children and reach our *Real-Time Parenting* vision. We enhance our connection with our child. As Gloria DeGaetano, founder of the Parent Coaching Institute emphasizes, "What you pay attention to grows."

YOUTUBE TOGETHER AS PART OF ROUTINE

 It is easy for parents' attention to move toward their children's devices and away from their children. Tamara is a parent who was struggling with day-to-day interactions with her children, ages six and twelve. Bedtime was especially difficult, starting with repeated requests to turn off YouTube videos and get ready for bed. After four or five requests (and Tamara's voice getting increasingly louder), the girls were still absorbed in videos. Next was the battle to brush teeth, get pajamas on, and choose a quiet time activity. Another round of repeated requests often ended up with Tamara yelling, the girls pouting, and no one getting to bed on time.

Tamara realized her need for quiet time to decompress from her day. She discovered the self-care pillar of parenting needed attention. She created a vision: a calm and effective bedtime plan. As Tamara began to focus on what was working and what was not, she pinpointed various elements of the routine. Tamara noticed what was happening in the moment when she asked the girls to turn off their videos.

She became aware of her feelings when they seemed to ignore her requests. Tamara paid greater attention to all that was going on in the evening and the ways the girls were getting her attention.

Tamara worked to become more observant and present in the evenings. She realized the YouTube videos were a distraction for the girls and delayed the start of the bedtime routine. The family decided to spend twenty minutes watching YouTube together once dinner was cleaned up and homework was completed. This allowed Tamara to be present with the girls, include the videos for a limited time, and help them transition to the bedtime routine.

Tamara also began to use descriptive language to help the girls stay motivated and on task. She would remark to her six-year-old, "You've got your teeth brushed and now you just need to get those pajamas on." Tamara described the parts of the routine that were on track, "You remembered to put your homework folder in your backpack! What else needs to go in with it?" This shift in focus and language helped Tamara stay positively engaged and connected with the girls. It helped the girls follow directions without repeated requests. Tamara felt great about the steps she took to create the plan for the evenings. She enjoyed cooperation and peace, and the efficient routine gave Tamara more time to enjoy her favorite podcasts once the girls were in bed.

Using descriptive language not only helps to build connections with our children, it also helps to encourage cooperation. We can describe what we see to reinforce desired behaviors and to respectfully address negative ones.

You are holding my hand to cross the street. This is how we stay safe.

Javier has his pants and shirt on. Ynez is getting her socks on. You guys look ready for school.

You saw that I was on the phone and waited for me to finish. Now I can talk with you.

Wow — you finished your homework and put it in your homework folder. That is what I call responsible!

Evan turned off his video game and came to the kitchen the first time I asked. I appreciate such good listening!

You remembered to put the car keys back on the hook. It is so nice to not have to search for them when I need to go out.

Children are typically more willing to accept descriptions rather than reprimands or lectures. And parents typically feel better about interactions when they replace this type of negative communication with positive reminders.

I see shoes all over the front hall. I am afraid someone will trip over them.

When I hear you use that tone of voice, I don't feel motivated to help you.

I see a half-finished math sheet and am worried about your effort in math.

It's hard to see you on your phone when you've been asked to help with dinner. I feel angry and annoyed.

When you didn't come home on time, I was scared something had happened to you.

Parents often wonder about the effectiveness of descriptive language. They wonder if they are letting their kids off the hook or handling them with kid gloves. In our work with thousands of parents, we have witnessed the opposite scenario.

An added benefit of descriptive language is that it helps parents stay present and mindful of the moment. Rather than moving back to past frustrations, *Why can't you ever …*, or racing forward to future concerns, *You will never be able to…*, we focus on the present moment. Concentrating on past behavior leads to playing the blame game. Jumping ahead to future concerns feeds our fears. The only time that matters is now. Use descriptive language to tune in to the child in front of you in real time.

It can be tricky to speak in a new way with our kids. Like any new habit, trying it out can feel awkward or disingenuous. And there are many ways to use words,

> **Parents experience a higher impact on their children's behaviors when they use direct, non-evaluative and honest communication.**

tone, and language. We encourage you to bring courage and curiosity to this new approach to conversation. Embrace words that are compelling to you. Practice a variety of ways to notice and describe behaviors. Be patient with yourself as you try out new ways to communicate. Find what works for you.

DESCRIBE RATHER THAN EVALUATE

 Take six note cards — three for positive feedback and three for negative. On one side of each card, write an evaluative statement. On the other side, write the descriptive statement in a neutral way.

Evaluative statement: You got an A on your paper. You are an awesome English student!

Descriptive statement: Looks like you got positive feedback on your English paper. You put a great deal of time and effort into that paper. What were some interesting things you learned?

Evaluative statement: You are such a slob! It's ridiculous that you still haven't learned to pick up after yourself.

Descriptive statement: Your shoes are blocking the front entry and your dirty dishes are in the kitchen sink. It is frustrating to come home and have to step over and work around the things you have left out. Please take care of this.

OFFER CHOICES

 It can be tricky to shift from trying to control behaviors to influencing behaviors. It takes intention and a shift in mindset. Offering choices is a simple yet powerful tool in this quest to encourage desirable behaviors. When children are invited to make a choice, they are building skills in decision making and developing their autonomy. Autonomy is an important developmental milestone that children build from birth to adulthood; making choices and learning from the results of those decisions is one of the best ways to develop autonomy.

Suppose your six-year-old continually jumps on the living room couch. You ask him again and again to stop, yet he continues to jump. Your repeated requests may have unintentionally given him attention for his inappropriate behavior. Instead, offer him two appropriate choices: "Jumping on the couch is dangerous. You can jump on the floor here in the living room or jump on the beanbag chair downstairs. You decide." By offering your six-year-old two choices, you invite him to make an appropriate choice, while still honoring his need to jump.

Offering choices helps to encourage cooperation. Parents are constantly giving their children directions.

Eat your breakfast.
Get dressed.
Brush your teeth.
Finish your homework.
Take out the garbage.
Be considerate to your sister.
Turn off the iPad.
Go to bed now.

It can feel overwhelming to a child. And they often tune us out. We can empower our children to make good decisions by offering them choices. Children are often more motivated when they have a say in the matter.

Would you like eggs or yogurt for breakfast?
Do you want to wear the blue shirt or the red shirt today?
Do you want to brush your teeth first, or wash your face first?
Are you planning to finish your homework before dinner or after dinner?
Please take out the garbage now or after your show ends.
Can you be in the same room with your sister, or do you need some space in your room?
You can turn the iPad off now or in five minutes.

Will you read books or listen to music before going to bed?

The choices we offer our children will likely reflect our values. Your family may feel fine with children jumping on the couch. One of the choices you offer may be deciding who gets to pick the Friday night movie. One family may provide choices regarding which clothing to wear, while another family is focused on which

Giving choices helps parents set boundaries while showing respect for the child.

bathroom to clean. Find what fits your values, your needs, and your *Real-Time Parenting* vision and action plan.

Offering choices may not always result in cooperation; we will look at additional techniques to foster cooperation in the problem-solving section in Chapter 6. Yet, coming up with two viable options before giving a direction can be extremely effective.

GIVE CLEAR AND FIRM DIRECTIONS

 Many parents fall into a few bad habits that interfere with communication. Be aware of common communication traps and mindful of the message you intend. The first trap is do not imply that your child has a choice when there isn't one. It sounds subtle, but there is a clear difference between "How about picking up your toys now?" and "It is time to pick up your toys." We are just as kind, yet clear and firm, when we avoid phrasing directions as a question. Avoid adding "okay" to your directions. "Please brush your teeth now," is kind yet more effective than "Please brush your teeth, okay?"

The second communication trap is unconsciously creating a threat by using "if" with a negative consequence. This may help a child cooperate, yet it does not show respect for the relationship, nor does it encourage cooperation. In addition, using "if" with your directions may imply the child has a choice.

If you don't get your pajamas on right now, we won't be able to read books.
If you don't get your homework finished, you will not get to watch the game on TV tonight.
If you don't turn off your video game by 8:00 p.m., you can't play at all tomorrow.
If you are late, no car for you next weekend.

Consider using "when" followed by a positive outcome rather than "if" followed by a negative consequence. The clarity and directness of the "when" statements encourage a positive response rather than a power struggle for both parent and child.

When you get your pajamas on right away, we will have time for two books before bed.
When you finish your homework, you will be able to watch the game on TV.
You can play your video game an hour tomorrow when you remember to turn off your game by 8:00 p.m. today.
When you return home by curfew, you can use the car again next weekend.

Over-using the word "no" is a third communication trap. Parents often have to deny their child's request; however, finding alternative words can help influence positive behavior. Many parents respond to their children with a quick "no."

No, you can't have a cookie right now. It's almost dinner time!
No, you can't stay up later tonight!
No, you cannot order that from Amazon!

Many parents have felt better about connection and cooperation when they rephrase their response.

A cookie will be right over here for you after dinner.
Staying up later would be fun for the weekend.

That looks cool. Would you like to add it to your birthday gift list?

SET UP THE PHYSICAL SPACE TO FIT YOUR GOALS

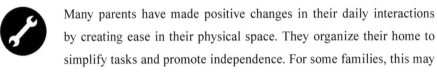 Many parents have made positive changes in their daily interactions by creating ease in their physical space. They organize their home to simplify tasks and promote independence. For some families, this may mean creating a place for healthy snacks that children can easily access. For other families it may mean adding stools in the bathroom to help children reach toothpaste. It may mean adding storage space to reduce clutter or revamping technology space to improve supervision. Take a closer look at your home environment. Are there changes that would build independence, reduce conflict, and promote cooperation?

Sara and Anwar were having difficulty getting their children to listen to them and cooperate with family expectations. One of their ongoing power struggles was repeated requests to keep track of their belongings. Sara and Anwar would often look around their home after a long day to find shoes and coats strewn around the family room as well as backpacks spilling their contents onto the stairs.

Through coaching, Sara and Anwar chose to focus on the pillar of rituals and routines. They realized they needed a better setup for storing coats and backpacks. They noticed their own shoes were often blocking the entry.

They worked with their kids to reorganize their closet space. They added extra hooks for coats and backpacks and racks for shoes. The four of them made a commitment to one another to consistently use their newly designed space. Conflicts over belongings diminished. Sara and Anwar shifted the negative interactions in their home by changing the environment.

Megan and Brandt were early risers and liked to go to sleep by 9:00 p.m. They took turns staying up to enforce a 10:00 p.m. curfew on their 14-year-old daughter's YouTube and social media accounts and ended up resenting their daughter for their lost sleep. Megan and Brandt were overjoyed when they installed a router they could set to prevent any internet use after 10:00 p.m. They could sleep knowing their daughter's curfew was enforced through the physical environment.

ESTABLISH EFFECTIVE ROUTINES

Effective daily routines also lead to positive behaviors. Routines provide a structure that helps children feel safe and secure. You may not even realize you have a routine until you stop and observe what is currently going on in your home. How did you rate yourself when you considered the routine pillar in Chapter 3? Do you aspire to create change in this area? Would it help to clarify your desires and goals for your routines?

Let's take another look at Jennifer and her three children, who implemented changes to get to the school bus on time. By shifting her attention and using descriptive language, Jennifer and her three kids were experiencing more peaceful mornings. Yet Lilly, age seven, needed additional help staying focused on her morning tasks. Jennifer aspired to create a better routine with Lilly.

Parents mean well when they present their children with schedules or routines, yet kids do better with a plan that they have helped create. Jennifer shared her observations about the current situation and asked Lilly to brainstorm a list of the things she needed to do each morning to be ready for school. They discussed what needed to be done first and what things could be done later. They talked about the time needed for each task and finalized Lilly's morning routine. Lilly's routine consisted of ten tasks, beginning with "get dressed" and ending with "hug mommy." (It helps to include some easy or fun tasks!)

Next, they decided to create a simple picture chart to help with consistency. They put the chart on the kitchen counter each morning, with colorful beads on each task. As Lilly completed the tasks, she moved the beads from the chart to a jar. This simple action helped reinforce the habit. Lilly took responsibility to do the task and enjoyed moving her beads from the chart to her jar. When the jar was full, Jennifer and Lilly made necklaces with the beads, an added bonus! Lilly became more independent, and the family enjoyed the order and calm of the improved morning routine.

There are many ways to influence behavior and improve interactions. Consider the underlying need that may be driving the behavior. Look for opportunities to encourage the behaviors that align with your family values and with your *Real-Time Parenting* vision. Experiment with descriptive language and offer choices. Take a closer look at your physical space and your daily routines to see what improvements are possible.

CREATE ROUTINES FOR YOUR UNIQUE FAMILY

Choose one of your daily routines—morning routine, dinner time, homework time, bedtime—whichever one may need a little attention. Think about what happens now. Close your eyes and imagine this daily routine. Answer the following questions.

Current routine:
- Where does this routine occur?
- How is the space currently set up for the family during this time?
- Who is involved in this routine?
- What is each person typically doing during this time?
- What are you typically doing during this time?

Now imagine your ideal routine:
- How is the space set up?
- What are family members doing in your ideal scenario?

- What are you doing?
- Are there days currently when your ideal routine happens?
- What helps support your ideal routine?

Creating your routine in real time:
- Do you need to change your timing for this routine?
- What steps might you take to alter the space?
- How can you encourage family members to engage in ways that align with your ideal?
- Are there ways to make your routine more enjoyable?
- Note ideas listed that you are ready to work on today.

We encourage you to have an open mind as you test out the seven tools we have introduced thus far. You may notice your spouse or partner feels more comfortable with one skill while you prefer another. We encourage you to remain curious and open as you find what works for your vision. And as always, be patient and gentle with yourself as you work to make positive changes.

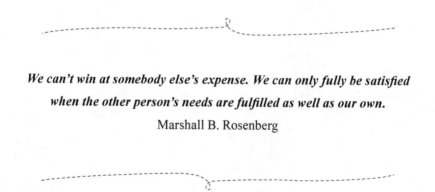

We can't win at somebody else's expense. We can only fully be satisfied when the other person's needs are fulfilled as well as our own.
Marshall B. Rosenberg

6

DISCIPLINE MEANS TEACHING RESPONSIBILITY

In this chapter, we invite you to explore:

- Methods to establish rules and follow through with them
- A framework for addressing difficult behavior in a respectful way
- Ideas for solving the most challenging problems

We introduced tools in previous chapters to strengthen your relationship with your child and positively influence their behavior. We realize parents often need additional tools for discipline — especially when these front-end tools require some backup actions. We now explore four additional tools for your toolkit: establish effective routines, set rules and follow through with them, use appropriate consequences, and solve problems together.

While some think of discipline as punishment, we refer to discipline as the clear steps taken to teach and reinforce learning. It is derived from the Latin word *disciplina* meaning "instruction given, teaching, learning, knowledge." When parents come to coaching for discipline tools, we encourage them to focus on teaching rather than punishing. We support discipline techniques that address safety and responsibility while enhancing the parent-child relationship.

Many parents argue that "punishment works to force a child to obey" and, quite frankly, they are often correct. Doling out punishment can alter a child's behavior in the moment. However, punishment can have negative long-term effects on children. Jane Nelsen shares the drawbacks of the "Four R's of Punishment":

Resentment — *This is unfair. I can't trust adults.*

Revenge — *They are winning now, but I'll get even.*

Rebellion — *I'll do just the opposite to prove I don't have to do it their way.*

Retreat — *I won't get caught next time* (sneakiness) or *I am a bad person* (reduced self-esteem).

Nelsen poses the question, "Where did we ever get the crazy idea that in order to make children do better, first we have to make them feel worse?" When children are strictly punished, the experience tends to produce anger, fear, or resentment rather than inspire learning and responsibility.

We encourage parents to implement discipline strategies that align with the authoritative parenting approach we introduced in Chapter 1. A combination of parental guidance with child participation is more effective than attempting to manipulate and control children. Effective discipline teaches children responsibility and accountability. It helps children develop respect for themselves, their families, their peers, and the community at large. The results include not only better behavior, but enhanced learning and a deeper parent-child connection.

Effective discipline teaches children that actions have consequences. Children learn to control their own behavior by making choices, wrestling with mistakes, and taking responsibility for their actions. Effective discipline helps children become resilient adolescents and adults who make good decisions for themselves.

Discipline involves providing structure, order, firm boundaries, and age-appropriate expectations. Effective discipline keeps children safe and teaches important family rules and life skills.

WHOSE BUSINESS IS IT?

Parents can respond more effectively to discipline situations when they consider the issue and who truly **owns** it. Does the issue belong to the child? Can the parent support his child without interfering? In *The Art of Positive Parenting,* Mickey Tobin defines a problem that belongs to the child as one that "does not interfere with your rights or dignity or with health and safety." If the problem is the child's business, simply responding with intentional listening is your best approach.

Or does the problem belong to the parent? Does it cause a negative impact on the parent's rights or dignity, or put the child's health or safety at risk? Using descriptive language in addition to listening when addressing these situations may be more effective. And if your child needs additional reinforcement to control their behavior, a discipline technique might be in order.

Deciding whether an issue truly belongs to your child is a necessary starting point to determine what parenting skills are needed. If you determine the behavior is only impacting the child, does not interfere with the parent's rights or dignity, and does not put the child's health or safety at risk, step back and allow your child to navigate the situation. Listen attentively to support the child's process of coming up with his own response. Provide opportunities for your children to practice and build problem-solving skills. Honor their experiences — triumphs or failures. Both types of experiences help children develop responsibility and grow into knowledgeable, capable, and resilient adults.

> When it is your child's business, step back to foster respect and independence.

Let's take a closer look with some examples. Whose business is it?

1. Your four-year-old is frustrated with his Legos.
2. Your seven-year-old isn't invited to a classmate's birthday party.
3. Your ten-year-old is disruptive or overly messy at the dinner table.
4. Your twelve-year-old is cut from the travel team.

5. Your fifteen-year-old is watching porn.

If you decided that situations 1, 2, and 4 are your child's business, we would agree. Intentional listening is all that is needed as an effective response. As you notice and name your child's feeling, you might say:

It makes you mad when you can't find the Lego piece you need.

It is so disappointing that you weren't invited to the party.

You were hoping to make the team — how upsetting!

Situation 3 interferes with the parent's right to a reasonable dinner time. Situation 5 puts the child's health and safety at risk. These two issues that belong to the parent can be addressed with additional tools which we will discuss later in this chapter.

WHOSE BUSINESS IS IT? (PART ONE)

 Think about your day-to-day interactions with your kids. What are some common problems that arise in real time?

1. Grab a stack of note cards. Think of eight to ten behavioral issues. Jot each issue down on a separate card.

2. Look at each card. Read the issue. Does it involve the rights and dignity of others? Health or safety? If the answer is no, these issues belong to your child. Place them in the "Child" pile. If the issue involves health and safety or the rights and dignity of others, the parent needs to get involved, so put these in the "Parent" pile. If the issue seems like it might involve both parent's business and child's business, start a "Both" pile. We will look at the "Parent" pile and the "Both" pile later, so set those aside for now.

3. Take the "Child" pile with issues that belong to your children. Read each issue

again. Can you step back? Can you let them control their own business? If so, intentional listening is your best tool. On the back of each card, write a possible listening response. Look back to Chapter 4 if you need a refresher on ways to intentionally listen.

4. After practicing this activity, reflect on the following questions:
- What do you notice about your child as you let him take care of his own business? What do you notice about yourself?
- How does letting go of control show respect for your child?
- How does it help you reach your vision?

SET RULES AND FOLLOW THROUGH

Respect and responsibility are the two values we hear about most often as parent coaches. Parents universally want children to respect others and show responsibility for their actions. When they model respect for themselves and others, parents set the stage for children to learn to show respect and take responsibility.

A primary way parents teach responsibility is to clearly state and follow through with rules. This can be difficult for many families, especially when parents have different values and parenting styles. Even when Mom and Dad do the work to get on the same page, they may be faced with a new stage of development that requires new insights and rules. Or, perhaps Mom and Dad have come up with a great set of rules — yet don't have the proper tools to reinforce them.

As parents put their *Real-Time Parenting* vision into action, they often need real-time rules. We encourage you to think about what rules would be helpful for your family. Remember that each family is different — there is no one set of rules that works for all families. When considering rules, start by creating as few as possible. Keep them clear and simple. It can also be extremely effective to get input from your children when creating rules for your family. Invite your children to discuss rules and listen to their ideas. Ideally, you will design rules as a team. When kids have a voice in the discussion and some ownership of the plans of action, they tend to demonstrate greater cooperation and accountability.

Follow-through is essential — yet this can be the hardest part! We get distracted with our own devices and let our kids linger on theirs long past the agreed time limit. We are tired after a long day of work and decide it is easier to let the kids stay up rather than stick with our bedtime rule. Or perhaps we are feeling stressed and choose to do our child's chore for them rather than risk a confrontation. Be aware of what gets in the way of following through.

Once your rules are established, give clear reminders, and follow through!

THE IMPORTANCE OF FOLLOW-THROUGH

Nine-year-old Rebecca hated wearing her bike helmet. She'd often take off down the driveway, leaving her helmet behind. When her mom, Anne, saw her without a helmet, she would tell Rebecca that she would not be allowed to ride her bike for two days. Yet when the next day would come and Rebecca would tell her mom about an invitation to ride with a friend, Anne decided to avoid a confrontation and let Rebecca go. Rebecca had not learned to take responsibility for her own safety.

Rebecca's friend and neighbor, Ellie, had the same rule about wearing a bike helmet, which had been clearly stated for years. When Ellie left her house without her helmet, she lost the privilege of riding her bike the next day. Because Ellie's mom has routinely followed through, Ellie rarely left the house without her helmet. The clear rule — plus mom's follow-through — helped teach Ellie that she must wear a helmet whenever she rides her bike.

Follow-through can look different for different parents. Sometimes follow-through is simply feedback — a comment to appreciate a positive choice or to redirect a behavior. Sometimes follow-through includes validating your child's feeling. You may acknowledge his disappointment regarding a rule, yet still maintain your expectation. Other times, follow-through entails taking an action to reinforce a rule or limit.

USE APPROPRIATE CONSEQUENCES

When we talk about following through, we are often referring to consequences. There are two types of consequences that encourage children to take responsibility for their behavior: natural and logical. Natural consequences are those that happen naturally without interference from a parent. Examples are a child whose markers dry up because he forgets to replace the cap or a teen who can't wear her jeans to a party because they didn't make it into the laundry. Logical consequences are outcomes related to the misbehavior that have been planned ahead of time and are carried out by the parent. Some examples are taking away a phone if the child is misusing an app or separating children who are hitting each other.

Whenever possible, we suggest that parents allow natural consequences to teach children about what occurs as a result of their choices. Parents give a clear message that their child is responsible for himself when he experiences natural consequences. This is a respectful way to teach responsibility. Relationships are better served when life teaches the lesson — when children experience the naturally occurring results. Parents encourage their children to make choices and learn from successes or failures, rather than impose their control over them. When parents focus on natural consequences, they step back and allow their child to be accountable for their own business, while being present to listen and support.

José, age four, throws his bath toys out of the tub and has no more toys to play with during his bath.

Emily, age eight, forgets to pack her snack for school. Her hunger lasts until lunch time.

Sean, age twelve, forgets to study for his math test. He gets a lower grade than he had hoped.

Anna, age fifteen, doesn't take her coat to the football game. She is cold during the game and leaves early.

It can be difficult to stand back and let nature take its course.

José pleads and cries for his parents to retrieve his toys. His parents remain polite yet firm. They know he will have a chance to play with his toys during his next bath. They are teaching José a real-time lesson that is best learned by experiencing the consequences of his actions.

Emily is irritated that she didn't get to eat a snack and blames Mom when she gets home from school, "Why didn't you remind me to pack my snack?" Mom remains polite but firm, "I am sorry you were hungry at snack time. What ideas do you have so you will remember your snack tomorrow?"

Sean is disappointed that he did not get the grade he was hoping to achieve.

Anna feels cold and uncomfortable at the game.

Life teaches the lesson.

CONNECT CONSEQUENCES TO SPECIFIC BEHAVIOR

There are times when allowing life to teach the lesson is not safe or realistic. Ellie and her bike helmet are an example. The natural life lesson (getting hurt without a helmet) would put her in danger; therefore, Mom steps up and imposes a logical consequence. Losing the privilege of riding her bike logically follows the behavior.

A logical consequence is one that a parent imposes. Children learn important lessons when the consequence relates to the situation in a sensible way. Parents can teach their children life lessons by expecting them to amend a situation with words or deeds. Lessons are typically more effective when parents are fair, firm, and consistent with their follow-through. Ideally, the consequences have been discussed and understood prior to enforcing them. If the family has worked together to agree on the consequences, they are even more effective.

Four-year-old Tommy throws his toy in anger. The natural consequence might result in the toy breaking, yet Tommy's parents want to teach him responsibility and safety. A logical consequence follows: the toy is put on a shelf and Tommy can play with it again tomorrow.

Kevin, age ten, often gets upset that his older brother is more skilled when building with K'nex. When Kevin knocks over his brother's structure, his father asks Kevin to make amends by helping to rebuild it.

Grace, thirteen, borrows her mother's nail polish and carelessly spills it on the tile floor. Grace's mother accepts her apology and requires her to clean up the spill.

Sixteen-year-old Rana has a 10:30 p.m. curfew. She arrives home at 10:55 p.m. Mom and Dad remind Rana of the rule and let Rana know she will be grounded at home next Saturday evening.

Logical consequences should be age appropriate and time sensitive. For example, four-year-old Tommy loses the toy for one day and can try again tomorrow. If his parents waited a week to give him another chance, the lesson would be lost. Older children have a greater sense of time and a better understanding of cause and effect. A middle-schooler may need a week to learn from a consequence, a teenager perhaps longer.

Parents often ask us about losing privileges. It stands to reason that providing a logical consequence is very similar to losing a privilege. The key here is the logic involved. Does it make sense for Aldo to lose his dessert because he hit his brother? Does the consequence logically follow the behavior? Perhaps time in his room, separated from his brother, is a more meaningful, logical consequence for Aldo. Should Maria lose her phone privileges because she failed to take the dog out? Does phone usage directly relate to walking the dog? Perhaps Maria should be expected to do an extra chore to make up for the one she missed.

Logical and natural consequences help children learn about themselves and the world around them. Sometimes they learn about the results of their actions. Other times they learn how to understand and regulate their emotions. Parents who use appropriate consequences teach their children about choices and outcomes in a consistent and respectful manner. Some parents may use slightly different consequences for different children in their family. Because each child is unique, we encourage parents to find the consequences that are meaningful for each individual child.

DIFFERENT CONSEQUENCES FOR DIFFERENT CHILDREN

Juan and Sofia came to coaching because they were looking for better ways to manage their son's angry outbursts. As they gained a better understanding of their values, they honed in on their desire to be respectful of individual differences. When their older son, Alexi, became upset or didn't follow the rules, he was required to go to his room. He usually did this as instructed. The time in his room gave him some solitude and a chance to calm down.

He was able to regulate his emotions and return to the family. Sending Alexi to his room felt effective for him and his parents.

When their younger son, Carlos, became upset or had trouble following rules, Juan and Sofia tried sending him to his room. Yet, they discovered that sending Carlos to his room only intensified the situation. Because Carlos hated being alone, a power struggle ensued that involved frustration and yelling from Mom and Dad, and anger and tears from Carlos. To make matters worse, the fear of being alone in his room only intensified Carlos' emotions. Juan and Sofia were inspired to be flexible and find alternatives for his tantrums. They realized that he was better able to calm down and regroup when one of his parents simply sat down with him. The expectation to calm down and rejoin the family was consistent for both boys, yet the method to comfort and teach calming down was slightly different.

> A soft landing provides a supportive environment for children to learn important life lessons from their mistakes.

PROVIDE A SOFT LANDING

Have you noticed how discipline requires insight and flexibility as compared to punishment? The consequences are sensible and meaningful. They are unique to each family and sometimes to each child. We provide a soft landing when we refrain from using roadblocks, such as shaming or blaming the child. Instead, we provide follow-through while maintaining connection with the child. And there is always room for compassion after a child experiences a consequence. Parents can remain a loving presence while stepping back and letting the child handle his or her own business.

Many parents attempt to discipline by taking away important privileges or special events. They believe missing a meaningful event will teach their child the appropriate behavior. A child hits his brother and loses the chance to attend his best friend's birthday party. Is this a logical result of his actions? He may learn not to hit, but he may also get the idea that his parents are mean and unfair. Or he may feel so distraught that he is unable to process the message. We encourage matching the impact of the consequence to the behavior. A friend's birthday, a special family outing, or a school dance may happen just a few times a year. Ideally, parents can find a more reasonable consequence to do the teaching so the special event can still be enjoyed. Parents can provide firm consequences that feel fair and respectful.

Earning privileges rather than taking them away is another way to provide fair, firm, and respectful consequences. Rather than losing a privilege, give children an opportunity to gain one. Instead of the parent controlling the situation by handing down a consequence, the child takes responsibility for the situation and earns a privilege. When parents shift the focus, situations often move from a negative interaction to a positive one.

A BEDTIME SHIFT

 Andrea was tired at the end of her workday and looked forward to connecting with her girls in the evening. She loved to spend time cuddling and reading with them, yet bedtime had become a nightmare. When Andrea repeatedly asked her daughters to brush their teeth and get their pajamas on, she was met with rambunctious behavior and noncompliance. She then began to threaten her girls to try to get them to listen. "If you don't get your pajamas on now, we will not have time to read books." And after another few threatening reminders, "That's it! No books tonight!" This was followed by further negotiation and often tears. All parties felt lousy when it was time to say goodnight. There was not only negativity and tension, but Andrea missed reading with her daughters.

Through our coaching process, Andrea shifted the focus from losing books to gaining them. She told her girls, "When you get your teeth brushed and your pajamas on the first time I ask, we will have time to read a third book tonight." If the girls started to dawdle, Andrea reminded them, "There is still time for two books. I know you will get those pajamas on quickly!" Shifting the consequence from a negative one to a positive one helped everyone feel more motivated. The girls followed the routine most nights, and Andrea enjoyed spending time reading with her girls.

Whether the situation is best handled with a natural consequence or a logical one — or by losing or gaining a privilege — it is vital to start with connection. Listen first. Validate the feelings involved. Remember that you can listen to feelings and provide validation even if you do not agree with the message. Provide a firm consequence and offer a soft landing to support your child as he learns from his mistakes. And, most importantly, find an approach that works for you, your child, your values, and your vision.

Think about how you are currently using consequences. Are they working for you? Are your children learning from the natural events that follow their actions? Are they learning from consequences you impose that logically follow their behavior? Do your consequences align with the message you would like to convey? Do they align with your family values? Do they help meet your vision? Would it help to create an action plan that incorporates effective consequences?

RULES, CHOICES, AND FOLLOW-THROUGH

When we work with parents in private coaching or group classes, we are often asked about discipline. Parents are looking for alternatives to nagging, yelling, and ineffective punishment. They often focus on the discipline pillar and create a vision for change. We teach a process for using discipline techniques in real time. Effective discipline includes providing choices for children that help them feel empowered to have some control over the situation. We refer to this as: Rule-Choice-Follow-through, or R-C-F.

When disciplining our children in real time, it is helpful to state the rule, offer a choice, and follow through with them. This process gives parents a three-part action plan for accountability. The **rule** is clearly stated, providing structure and limits for the child. The parent offers a **choice** which supports both cooperation and autonomy. This gives children practice in making positive choices and taking responsibility for their actions. The parent then **follows through** with meaningful comments or consequences. The follow-through may be words of appreciation to reinforce a positive choice. The follow-through may be a logical consequence from the choice the child has made. The follow-through is the action parents take in response to their child's choice and helps to teach children about the effects of their choices.

R-C-F is especially effective when parents first use encouragement and replace roadblocks with intentional listening. Providing structure, creating a supportive home environment, and establishing effective routines are additional front-end strategies that help to improve the effectiveness of R-C-F.

Sari, age three, tries to run when her mother takes her out of her car seat. Mom takes her hand and responds using R-C-F. "Sari, you need to be safe and stay with me in this parking lot." (**Rule**) You can hold my hand, or I will carry you." (**Choice**) Sari tries to squirm away. Mom picks her up and says, "It looks like you are choosing to be carried." (**Follow-through**)

Dylan, age seven, repeatedly grabs a toy from his four-year-old brother. Dad uses R-C-F. "Dylan, we take turns with toys." (**Rule**) "You may ask your brother for a turn or find another toy to play with for now. You decide." (**Choice**) Dylan picks up a different toy. Dad says, "That looks like a fun choice." (**Follow-through**)

Koko, age twelve, is begging her parents to go out to a movie with her friends. Her father uses R-C-F to address the situation. "Mom and I like to have a trusted adult nearby when you are at the movies with your friends. (**Rule**) "We will drive you and your friends and sit in the back of the theater. Or you can invite the girls to our house to watch a movie." (**Choice**) After much discourse about how embarrassing it would be to have her parents in the theater, Koko decides to invite the girls to watch a Netflix movie. Her parents stay firm with the options they have given Koko. (**Follow-through**) They order pizza and spend the evening in another part of the house while the girls enjoy their movie.

Miquel, age sixteen, goes to a party at the nearby college without his parents' permission. His parents discover this by seeing a picture that one of his friends posted on Instagram. They utilize R-C-F to discuss the infraction with Miquel. "We expect you to tell us where you are when you are out on the weekends." (**Rule**) "You can choose to tell us, or we will install a location app on your phone. What is going to work for you?" (**Choice**) Miquel balks at adding the app to his phone and promises to communicate openly about his evening plans by talking ahead of time or by texting in the moment. "You will need to stay home next Saturday night and then we will try again with the expectation that you will be open about where you are on the weekends." (**Follow-through**)

It can be difficult to come up with appropriate choices in real time. However, as parents experiment with this framework, they become more comfortable and skillful at offering choices. It can look very different for different families — as rules, choices, and follow-through are dependent upon what works for you. Keep in mind the importance of staying connected with your child using attentiveness and intentional listening as you use discipline techniques.

Intentional listening can be an especially important tool during the R-C-F approach. Sari might whine as Mom carries her across the parking lot. Mom can be firm with her follow-through yet empathize with Sari, "You would rather walk on your own." Dylan might express his frustration that his little brother always gets to play with the Ninja warrior. Dad validates his feelings before he offers a choice, "It is frustrating that you both want to play with the same toy." Koko's parents stay clear and firm about their rule regarding adult supervision at the movie, yet they understand their daughter's feelings. As Koko complains about the rule while mulling over her choice, her parents use intentional listening "It's embarrassing that your parents aren't ready for you to be at a movie without adults. You wish you could go without us." Miquel's parents may also use intentional listening, "It's tempting to do college type activities when you're still in high school. You feel ready for that freedom." Parents can acknowledge the child's point of view and still follow through with necessary boundaries or expectations. We can give our children permission to feel without giving them permission to behave in unacceptable ways. R-C-F is the framework that helps us teach our kids responsibility while we respect their feelings and uphold the family rules.

REPLACE TIME-OUT WITH TIME-IN

Michael, an active eight-year-old with high energy, would abruptly move from one activity to another. When asked to turn off his video game, he would often kick furniture or slam doors. His parents tried using a time-out chair when this occurred. They hoped sitting in the time-out chair would interrupt the negative outburst and give Michael space to calm down. Yet Michael was resistant to the time-out chair; he would raise his voice, twist his body, or run away. Directing him to sit in the chair seemed to escalate his misbehavior.

During the coaching process, Michael's parents shared how desperately they wanted Michael to slow down and control his impulses. They realized that trying to get Michael to sit in the time-out chair was frustrating and ineffective. They were trying to control his behavior. Instead, they wanted Michael to learn self-control. Through coaching, they came up with a new approach — a time-in corner.

Michael's parents introduced the time-in corner as an opportunity for Michael to manage his own behavior. They invited him to create the time-in corner with them. Together, they put a special blanket in the corner of his bedroom, added some pillows and his fidget spinner. They explained that this was his place to go when he needed to calm down. He could sit with his blanket and pillows and use his fidget spinner to calm himself. They created clear guidelines about the time-in corner. Michael would go on his own when needed. Other times his parents would ask him to go to regroup.

Michael's parents were thrilled with this new arrangement. There were some ups and downs, but Michael eventually began to utilize his time-in corner. After several weeks of persistent reminders, Michael began to find comfort in knowing he had a place to take a break. The difficult interactions were handled in a calm and effective manner. The time-in corner seemed helpful rather than punitive. Michael's parents helped him manage his frustration and regulate his emotions by providing the physical and emotional space he needed. Providing this type of space is another method to provide a soft landing.

Time-in spaces will look and feel different for different children. Another name for this type of space is a calming corner. Or you could give it any name that suits your family. We know that some children respond better using fidgets or tactile materials for comfort. You may want to include a soft blanket, a bumpy ball, or a box of cotton balls. Other children need quiet activities such as books or music to calm themselves. Or your child may need subtle movement to help calm himself — a box of Legos or a Rubik's Cube may help. The idea is to provide a technique that works for your child and is comforting, but not overly stimulating.

WHOSE BUSINESS IS IT? (PART TWO)

Review your notecards from Part One. You have three piles of behavioral issues labeled "Child," "Parent," and "Both." We suggest intentional listening as the best option when issues belong to your child. Listening helps a child feel supported and demonstrates trust that the child can manage her own business.

1. Now consider the "Parent" pile. (Set aside the third "Both" pile for now.) These are issues that involve the health and safety of your child or the rights and dignity of others and require parent intervention or a discipline technique. Review this pile to confirm that these issues belong in your "Parent" pile.

2. Imagine which discipline technique you might use to address these issues and jot your idea on the back of each card. Possible discipline tools include:

- Offer a choice to encourage cooperation
- Give a clear and firm direction so that you and your child understand the expectation
- Set up the physical space so that it fosters cooperation

- Establish an effective routine to clarify expectations and promote follow-through
- Set a rule and follow-through using R-C-F
- Use an appropriate consequence – consider whether a logical or natural consequence would be effective

We looked at five examples when we discussed *whose business is it* earlier in this chapter. We recommended using intentional listening for the three issues that belong to the child: a child frustrated with his Legos, a child who didn't receive an invitation to a birthday party, and a child cut from the travel team. Now that we have discussed additional discipline techniques, let's take a closer look at the other two scenarios. The ten-year-old who exhibits poor manners at the dinner table may be infringing upon his parent's right to have a pleasant meal. R-C-F is an option. The fifteen-year-old who is looking at porn may be handled using intentional listening and descriptive language in an honest discussion about safety, values, and the dangers of the Internet. Parents may also need to set firm rules and impose logical consequences such as limiting the use of devices or installing better parental controls.

SOLVE PROBLEMS TOGETHER

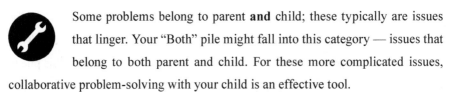 Some problems belong to parent **and** child; these typically are issues that linger. Your "Both" pile might fall into this category — issues that belong to both parent and child. For these more complicated issues, collaborative problem-solving with your child is an effective tool.

When parents show confidence in their children's abilities to contribute to solutions, children feel respected. Providing guidance when solving problems together can help develop life skills such as responsibility, resilience, and independence. As you brainstorm possible solutions, accept all ideas before choosing a few to try. Devise a plan that everyone can live with. When kids get to collaborate and create a plan, they are typically more successful at following through with it.

WORKING TOGETHER AS A FAMILY

 Let's look at Shelly and Jim, parents of Cassandra, age twelve, and James, age fifteen. They came to coaching because they worried their current family dynamic around homework was counterproductive. Through coaching they gained clarity and tools to support their vision of raising children who are responsible with a strong work ethic. They decided to create a new plan.

Homework was becoming a frustrating issue. Shelly and Jim spent a great deal of time reminding their teenagers to get their homework done. This included repeated requests to put electronics away and start on homework. They would often threaten a punishment yet lacked follow-through. Mom and Dad felt annoyed and disrespected that their requests were not honored. Cassandra and James felt badgered.

Shelley and Jim decided to try collaborative problem-solving with Cassandra and James. They recalled from coaching conversations how this approach honors the children's right to be part of the problem-solving process and gives children practice to work through life's challenges. Shelley and Jim wanted to demonstrate the trust and confidence they had in Cassandra and James to improve the situation.

Shelley and Jim learned these problem-solving guidelines through coaching.

Set a time and place for the conversation.

Do not attempt this in the heat of the moment.

Define the problem or issue or disagreement.

Listen to each person's point of view.

Brainstorm possible solutions.

Write down every idea, or have your children write them down, to validate each one without judgment.

Agree on one solution to try and create a plan.

Decide which action steps each person will take and how each person will work toward the solution.

Plan to follow up and make adjustments as needed.

Set a time and place for the next conversation to talk about how the solution is working.

Shelley and Jim had a family meeting with the kids. They started by making a positive statement about both Cassandra and James regarding their schoolwork. They then shared their frustration about the homework routine. They asked Cassandra and James for ideas on how to better structure the evenings so that homework would be started without nagging or arguing. Cassandra shared that her friends were often on Snapchat in the early evening and she wanted to connect with them. James said that he needed some downtime between school activities and homework. Shelley and Jim shared that they value good study habits and a strong work ethic. They clarified their expectation for a homework routine, but that the work and resulting grades were Cassandra's and James's responsibility.

The family decided on a new routine. Cassandra and James could utilize thirty minutes of screen time before dinner. Once dinner was over, they would focus on homework, without their devices. Cassandra's plan was to do homework in the kitchen. James would complete his homework in the dining room, using his iPad as needed. Shelley and Jim would make sure the homework got started but would trust that the kids would be responsible for completing it. The family agreed to try this plan for a week and review it the following weekend.

WHOSE BUSINESS IS IT? (PART THREE)

Do you have a "Both" pile? If so, review the issues in this pile. Are they problems that persist? Are they issues that belong to both you and your child? Can you imagine working together to address them? If so, write "Solve problem together" on the back of these cards. If you now see that the situation can be addressed using one of the other ten tools, write that tool on the back of the card.

As we coach parents to strengthen their front-end approaches, they often find a decreased need for back-up discipline tools such as imposing logical consequences or time-out. And most parents are happy to have extra tools in their parenting toolkit. When parents are fair, firm, and consistent, they experience fewer power struggles, better connection, and more pleasant interactions with their children.

CLEAN SLATE THEORY

When effective discipline is imposed within a connected relationship, children are more likely to be motivated to make better choices in the future. And they typically feel secure and respected rather than shamed or judged. This is a critical difference between discipline and punishment. When a parent uses a punishing mindset, she says things like, "You are never going to Alex's house again," or "That's the last time I trust you with the car." We encourage you to start each day anew with your children. Offer do-overs. We refer to this as the clean slate theory. Let go of the frustration and anger from yesterday. Be open to the new possibilities that each day brings. Start the day with a clean slate.

We are giving our kids the tools that will enable them to be
active participants in solving the problems that confront them —
now, while they're at home, and in the difficult, complex world that awaits them.
Adele Faber and Elaine Mazlish

7

CHANGE HAPPENS ONE STEP AT A TIME

In this chapter, we invite you to explore:

- A process for aligning your best intentions with real-time action steps
- How to use the research on habits to make positive changes that last
- The big shift from reacting to responding in challenging situations

We have met with hundreds of parents who have learned a great deal about parenting but are stuck in the same frustrating ruts with their families. They have taken in lots of information but are unable to apply it in useful ways. They often come away empty handed for many reasons. It is human nature to resist change. It is not easy to see how new insights translate into new habits. Additionally, when the powerful emotions of parenting come into play, the stress reactions of fight, flight, or freeze kick in, leaving the most well-intentioned parent disappointed and distraught.

We believe it is the everyday moments — routines, conversations, and decisions — that define our parenting experience. Parenting is a pressure-filled, round-the-clock job. Our typical or automatic reaction may not achieve the desired results. Parents report power struggles which leave both parents and children feeling defeated and frustrated. In *Parenting from the Inside Out*, Siegel and Hartzell explain, "When emotional reactions replace mindfulness ... it is very unlikely that you will be able to maintain nurturing communication and connection with your child."

TRIGGER TRACKER

 Observe yourself over the next few days to discover stressful experiences which cause you to react abruptly and behave in ways that do not align with your parenting vision. These experiences are triggers. Each person's triggers are unique. Recall the parenting profile from Chapter 1. Triggers may stem from past experiences or occur when life is unfolding in ways that clash with your personality or values. Triggers usually bring up uncomfortable feelings about yourself or others, such as feeling out of control, inadequate, or misunderstood. The purpose of this exercise is to raise your awareness by tuning in to the feelings and thoughts that arise in your body and mind at the onset of a stressful event. With recognition of what's happening in real time comes an opportunity for growth. With practice, you can choose to respond to triggering situations in ways that support your vision for your family.

Notice your triggers in real time. When you feel yourself getting irritated about something with your family, make a mental or written note. What is the triggering event? What's happening in your body including feelings and physical sensations? What thoughts are running through your mind? What is your reaction? At the end of the day, take a few minutes to record and reflect on your experience. Brainstorm

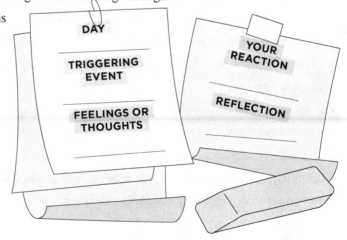

alternative responses. It's a practice do-over.

Be compassionate with yourself as you observe your triggers and behavior. Awareness is the necessary starting point for changing unwanted habits. Know that you don't have to settle for a cycle of negativity and power struggles. Choose one of the *Real-Time Parenting* tools to practice. You can make an intentional choice to break the cycle and create a better outcome.

STEP: SLOW DOWN, TUNE IN, EXPLORE OPTIONS, AND PROCEED

The *Real-Time Parenting* STEP model is a practical, effective way to integrate the important discoveries you have made into action. You have looked at your parenting profile and your unique child's needs. You have chosen the parenting pillars you want to improve and developed personal vision statements. You have learned ten parenting tools for creating change. STEP includes being mindful in the present situation and making intentional choices that align with your vision. STEP helps you bring your authentic action plan to life!

S - SLOW DOWN

Slowing down is a skill that many parents overlook. We are striving, reaching, rushing, scrambling, and doing multiple things at once. Our fast pace is fueled by a mental to-do list and thoughts of what needs to be done now and later.

Slowing down doesn't sound productive and it's not, from a mental doing perspective. It is human nature to rely mainly on our thinking mind to fix our problems. Sometimes the steady stream of thoughts is counterproductive. We ruminate. We spin stories of what should be. Give yourself a break from the mental churning and let go of trying to solve the entire problem immediately. Slow down and be in the present moment. Trust that this is an essential part of the process, even though it is messy and filled with uncertainty.

One way to shift the attention away from the whirling thoughts in your head is to tune in to your body, which reveals information beyond what the mind alone can tell us. Think of a camera lens zooming out as you let go of the thinking mind and listen to the messages coming from your body. Allow your feelings and reactions to be as they are. When we zoom out, we take a wider perspective of the situation and find breathing room.

Notice what happens in your body when you take a deep breath, imagine a pleasant scene, open a window, count to ten, or stroke your pet. Choose a slowdown method that works for you in any situation.

T - TUNE IN

Tuning in means considering what you know about yourself and your child in real time. How do you feel? What do you need? How might your child feel? What does your child need? This tuning in is a form of mindfulness. It is a process of stepping back. As Jon Kabat-Zinn said, "Even in our most trying, sometimes horrible moments as parents, we can deliberately step back and begin afresh, asking ourselves as if for the first time, and with fresh eyes, what is truly important here?"

Consider a parent yelling at his toddler for throwing food. What underlies the parent's frustration? Is it the mess? Is it the wasted food? Is it concern for the child getting enough to eat? All of these potential reasons are related to unmet needs of the parent, such as order, responsibility, and health.

> When we tune in, we can follow the wisdom and guidance that lies inside of us and discover what is truly important.

Just as we've been practicing recognizing feelings in our children, it is important to recognize feelings in ourselves. It may take time to uncover what we are truly feeling or needing in a situation. In other words, you may need to try on some different feelings until you land on the one that captures your inner experience. When we honor the importance of our underlying feelings and needs, we regulate ourselves and move forward in alignment with our parenting vision.

E - EXPLORE OPTIONS

Exploring options comes next. What is one thing you would like to change? What is possible? Start with some big questions. What action can I take to help bring this possibility to life? Is it a manageable task or action? Observe your energy and emotions as you ponder each option.

Recall your vision for your family. Which tool in your parenting toolkit will be most effective to meet your goals? Is this a situation where you need to uphold a rule? In this case, Rule-Choice-Follow-through is a good tool. Or, is it a situation that has persisted over time? Are your demands simply creating a power struggle? If so, sit down with your child and try solving the problem together. Is it a situation where your child simply needs you to be present as he processes what is happening? If so, practice intentional listening.

P - PROCEED

It's GO time! You have slowed down and noticed what is happening in your body. You have gained clarity by tuning in to feelings, thoughts, and information. And you have evaluated possible options to address the situation. Because you have done these three steps, you are now ready to take action. You are ready to **respond**, not react.

As you move through the STEP process, pretend you're a lab technician doing an experiment. Be curious and see how the situation unfolds without attachment to an exact outcome. Test out your action step to see what happens. Know that you will always be able to tweak, refine, or completely change course based on your observations.

You will be amazed at the results when you practice the STEP sequence and include it in your interactions. Over time you will experience less resistance and greater cooperation from your child. And most importantly your choices will enhance the connection between you and your child. The action you take may not result in a final resolution; you may even decide to try something different next time.

With practice, you will gain clarity and confidence in taking real-time action toward reaching your parenting goals.

STEP IN ACTION

One of the hardest things for parents to learn is how much to direct children as they navigate independence. How can we best support their learning and growth, and ensure they have the right balance of support and challenge for their development? When do we intervene — either by taking urgent action, giving a consequence, or working on a solution with our child — and when do we give our child space to wrestle with problems?

> The STEP process empowers parents to respond in a meaningful and effective way that aligns with their family vision.

We offer a framework to assist parents in deciding when to take the lead, when to collaborate with their child, and when to allow the child to take the lead in handling a given situation that arises. We have grouped many of the strategies and tools covered in the book into three categories — Step UP, Step WITH, and Step BACK. This framework helps parents make real-time decisions in an intentional way that aligns with their vision and the principles of authoritative parenting.

When a child's health or safety is threatened, we encourage parents to Step UP by providing important safety information and taking action to protect the child's physical or emotional well-being. Sometimes, parents need to act quickly to safeguard the child from an imminent threat. In other instances, parents can take time to formulate a plan for discipline.

When a child requires some caregiver assistance, such as a change in scenery, ideas to manage their behavior, or added structure to get through a situation, parents can Step WITH the child and be their guide.

When the child is capable of managing their own physical or emotional well-being, even if it is not the way a parent prefers it be managed, it is important to Step BACK. Resilience and problem solving are critical life skills, which can only be learned with adequate room for making and recovering from mistakes and learning from one's own experience.

The following charts are a guide for parents to use as they consider how to respond to their child's behavior.

STEP UP – PARENT LEADS	
Situation involves health and safety or rights and dignity of others	
3-year-old child hits baby	• Separate child from baby • State clear rule: gentle hands around baby; choice: you can play "peek-a-boo" or sing to baby or you can go to your calming spot • Follow through by walking child to calming spot or time-in corner if needed
8-year-old child refuses to wear a seatbelt	• Refuse to drive until seat belt is fastened • Give information about safety and laws • Consider where you can offer child a choice (which seat they sit in, radio station, window opened or closed, activity to do while driving)
13-year-old child breaks curfew on Saturday evening	• Decide on a logical consequence (lose privilege of going out next weekend) • Tell teen you were worried about their safety • Communicate the consequence and follow through with enforcing it • Problem solve with the child ways to make sure the curfew is not broken again

STEP WITH - PARENT AND CHILD COLLABORATE	
Situation involves a problem that belongs to both parent and child	
3-year-old cries and wants to leave large family event	• Consider child's unique temperament (slow to warm up socially) • Minimize loud/crowded/stressful events until child is better able to self-regulate • Provide child with breaks or shorten amount of time you attend important (or mandatory) events
8-year-old child angry at himself because of mistakes in his piano recital and wants to quit	• Acknowledge the child's feelings (disappointment or embarrassment) • Provide options for learning and development • Agree on a practice routine that works for the child and parent • Give clear expectations about committing to a specific time frame for lessons that is non-negotiable
13-year-old child struggles in school (has poor scores on two or more tests)	• Discuss what is challenging for the child • Listen to feelings and ideas of the child • Focus on any positive effort being made by the child • Adapt home routine to make sure there is adequate time/space for studying • Brainstorm a plan together such as getting extra help from a teacher or tutor or structuring study time • Put limits on activities that interfere with schoolwork such as social media

STEP BACK - CHILD LEADS	
Situation involves child's belongings, relationships, or responsibilities	
3-year-old is struggling to build his block tower	• Name the feeling of frustration or anger • Avoid building the tower for him • Give the child time to keep trying • Describe the child's effort
8-year-old child feels teased by a friend	• Listen to child as they process what happened • Refrain from intervening in child's relationship • Tell child you believe in her ability to handle the situation • Ask child what they would do differently next time
13–year-old child forgets sneakers for gym class again	• Tell child you are unable to bring them to school when they text you to bring the shoes • Allow natural consequence (child gets detention slip) • Listen briefly to child complain about what happened without blaming or shaming

Sometimes we need to make snap decisions as parents and sometimes we have the luxury of more time to decide on a response. You can use the STEP process in both types of situations.

DAD STEPS UP IN THE HEAT OF THE MOMENT

Jay had a strong sense of duty and family loyalty and wanted his boys to be the same way. This was challenging when his two sons, ages four and six, argued over the conflict du jour. Jay appreciated the logic of the STEP approach he had learned about at a *Real-Time Parenting* class. He realized his boys' arguing was a trigger for him because he feared his children would not look out for each other as they grew older. When his younger son started screaming at his brother for taking his spot on the family room couch, Jay felt the tension rising in his veins. He **slowed down** by counting to ten and **tuned in** to the fact that his sons were tired and hungry after a long day at school and after-care. He knew his usual tactics — yelling at the boys from the kitchen and threatening to take away their television time — were ineffective to stop the arguing. Jay decided to Step UP and test out a discipline strategy we discussed during the class. Because Jay had slowed down and tuned in, he was able to collect his thoughts and consider an action plan. (**Explore options and proceed**) He decided the Rule-Choice-Follow-through skill would be most effective for this situation.

Jay walked into the family room and stated, "You can watch TV together when you are using kind words with each other." (Rule) "You can both sit on the floor in front of the couch or you can come into the kitchen with me and help get dinner ready." (Choice) The boys moved to the floor and continued watching TV. Jay said encouragingly, "You'll be able to enjoy the show together now." (Follow-through) He returned to the kitchen.

Moments later, the arguing resumed. Jay returned to the family room and turned off the TV. He said very little as he walked the boys to the kitchen and gave each one a task to do. (Additional follow-through) Jay's actions had a powerful impact without interference from lecturing, arguing or blaming, or any other communication roadblocks.

MOM STEPS BACK DURING TEEN'S STRUGGLE

 When Josie picked Ava up from play practice, she could instantly tell her ninth-grade daughter was brooding over something. Ava slammed the door when she got into the car and barely grumbled hello in response to her mother's greeting. Josie wanted to know what was going on with Ava, but she had learned from experience that peppering her with questions would only cause her to shut down. Her vision was to have an open relationship with her teenage daughter. Josie waited and focused on calming herself down by listening to the song playing on the radio speakers. (**Slow down**) She recalled her recent conversations with her coach. Ava was adjusting to high school and developing her independence and identity as a young woman; she was very sensitive to her friends' comments and classmates' perceptions of her. (**Tune in**) Josie considered whether to comment or Step BACK and practice intentional listening. (**Explore options**) She lovingly grinned at Ava and began driving home quietly, trusting her daughter would eventually share what was troubling her. (**Proceed**)

During dinner, Ava commented that many kids weren't taking the play seriously and some were even vaping in the restroom before practice. Ava shared, "It was so annoying to watch the stupid director giving the high kids cues as if they were only having a hard time remembering their lines!" Josie caught her breath and thought to herself, *Ok so now she's opening up, don't blow it.* (**Slow down**) She noticed her stomach tightening and the fear she felt thinking of her daughter being pressured to start vaping. (**Tune in**) Josie wanted to launch into a lecture about the dangers of vaping. Yet she also recalled her last coaching session and the positive impact of listening with thoughtful presence, as well as encouragement and the importance of focusing on what's going well. (**Explore options**) She said to Ava, "That sounds really frustrating! You are taking play practice seriously and want others to do the same." (**Proceed**) Ava said, "Yeah, my friends and I aren't stupid enough to vape. We know it's dangerous and just last week a kid got caught and suspended for three days." Josie smiled as she replied, "It sounds like you've chosen a great group of friends, Ava!"

Sometimes parents use STEP over a longer time frame to respond thoughtfully to the situation. Notice how STEP helps keep the parent focused on what truly matters during a challenging time. It enables them to recall their vision for their family and put their thoughts and words into action.

FURY OVER FORTNITE

 DeAndre, age eleven, loved playing video games, and couldn't get enough of his favorite, Fortnite. Ben, DeAndre's father, came to parent coaching to address his fear that DeAndre was addicted to gaming and his grade point average was dropping. He showed no interest in homework and had gotten a low score on a recent math test. In frustration, Ben had talked and talked to DeAndre about the importance of good grades if he ever wanted to go to college. DeAndre only seemed to withdraw more from him in response. Ben was so angry about DeAndre's obsession with gaming that he was ready to throw the video console in the garbage.

Through parent coaching, Ben **slowed down** and took a wider perspective on the situation. He decided to find out why Fortnite captivated DeAndre. He sat down and watched him play. He noticed his son leading his teammates and cheering them on. He observed DeAndre's skills for strategizing and the confidence he showed as he progressed through the game. Ben shared that DeAndre even gave him a shy smile when he commented on how well he was playing. Ben **tuned in** to his feelings as he watched his son. He felt closer to DeAndre than he had in a long while. By simply learning more about his son's passion, he was making a connection.

Ben also recalled DeAndre's recent comments about his "horrible math teacher" and "idiot friends in their basketball jerseys." He found DeAndre's behavior was starting to make more sense. Why wouldn't he choose to focus on something he could excel at and win? Ben also realized his lectures only made DeAndre feel like more of a failure at math.

Next, Ben began **exploring options** during parent coaching. He brainstormed ways to help DeAndre academically. What would help DeAndre feel more confident as a student and around his peers? He considered offering to shift his evening schedule so he could be available to assist with math homework. Ben recalled how difficult algebra was for him in middle school, yet he had ended up working in the finance field. He recalled there was an after-school tutoring program at DeAndre's school, and he remembered how DeAndre used to enjoy going to the YMCA when he was in elementary school. He thought about learning more about gaming so he could talk to his son about it in a nonjudgmental way. Finally, he thought about setting up limits around when and how long DeAndre could be online gaming. Any one of these options would help move Ben toward his vision of raising a responsible, self-assured young man. Ben decided to Step WITH his son and **proceed**. He invited DeAndre to join him for a workout the following Saturday at the YMCA. Afterward, Ben planned to have a conversation with his son about building his math skills. He would give DeAndre the option of working with his father on math homework twice a week or going to the weekly tutoring program at school. Ben also committed to talking positively about DeAndre's passion for gaming.

BLUE LIGHT AT NIGHT

Tiffany came to parent coaching at her wit's end over her daughter Kayla's phone usage and sassy attitude. Bedtime had become a disaster. Kayla would sneak her phone under the covers and stay online texting her friends and watching YouTube videos instead of getting the sleep she needed. As a result, mornings were no better. Tiffany resorted to screaming and constant warnings for Kayla to get ready and not miss the school bus. Tiffany's vision was to have her rules taken seriously.

During parent coaching, Tiffany **slowed down** and became aware of the knot in her stomach and feelings of resentment. She disliked being the traffic cop when it came to monitoring Kayla's phone usage. The shouting and negative interactions on school days was taking a toll on her ability to get herself ready and focused for her

145

workday. She felt depleted and upset at how she and Kayla spent more time arguing than ever before. Above all, she missed the closeness she had once shared with her daughter at bedtime.

Tiffany **tuned in** to her frustration that the rules she had set for phone usage at bedtime weren't working. She wanted to feel competent as a parent. Tiffany also thought about her own phone usage and what she was modeling to her daughter. She recalled Kayla's irritation whenever she checked her work email or social media feed in the morning. Was this adding to the stress of getting them both out of the house on time? Tiffany also looked at the situation from Kayla's perspective. Kayla wanted control around using her phone and found ways to disregard the rules.

Tiffany **explored options** in parent coaching. She discovered she could use parental controls through the cell phone provider. She remembered hearing about an online tool from her pediatrician for calculating how much activity and rest a child requires based on their age. Lastly, she brainstormed ways to rebuild a connection with her daughter as she was entering adolescence. How could she have more relaxed evenings with Kayla?

Tiffany chose to Step UP and **proceed**. She set up parental controls. During dinner that evening, she showed Kayla the monthly wireless bill. She explained how Mom pays for them to have phone service each month and the company offers a tool to help parents ensure children are safe online and get the sleep they need. She told Kayla that the phone would be offline from 9 p.m. to 7 a.m. on weekdays and from 10 p.m. to 8 a.m. on weekends. Tiffany added that she was giving up her own phone usage in the mornings. She said she would stop checking her email and Instagram before Kayla left for school so she could be more relaxed getting them both ready for the day. While Kayla was annoyed by the new rules, it seemed to help that she wasn't the only one making changes. She even challenged her mom, saying, "This is going to be really hard for you!" Tiffany felt empowered about the new plan for managing screen time.

SOFT LANDING FOR HARD TIMES

 During a coaching session, Pooja shared a shocking experience she had with her son, Vinod. The teenager had come home from school in a foul mood. When Pooja asked him what was wrong, he let out a stream of complaints, punctuated by curse words, that left him breathless. He was furious at his teacher for accusing him of cheating on a test! Pooja was immediately triggered by her son's foul language and was aware of a creeping feeling of fear that her son had done something wrong. She remembered a key skill from parent coaching. She noticed her trigger and paused, allowing a few deep breaths to slow her down. She said nothing for a while and just stood in the room close to her son.

Pooja tuned in to Vinod's feelings of betrayal and disbelief that a teacher would call him out for something he didn't do. Pooja resisted verbalizing the questions that were flying through her head, Did you cheat? Why did your teacher think you cheated? Why are you being so disrespectful now? She knew that questioning would only make her son more defensive.

Pooja explored options as she considered her next response. Did Vinod need a reminder of the school policy? Isn't it a parent's job to correct him? She felt overwhelmed by Vinod's strong emotions. Pooja asked herself, *What does he need in this moment?* The words came to her and she proceeded. Showing understanding to her son, Pooja calmly said, "You want to be treated fairly." Vinod teared up when he looked at her and shook his head yes. His heavy breathing slowed down and he took a step closer to her. She put her arm on his shoulder, and he said, "I didn't do it, Mom. I was done with all the questions and just looked over to see how close Max was to finishing. I wanted to see if I was the first one done. Now I'm getting a big fat zero for the grade!" Another wave of thoughts hit Pooja as she listened to her son. *Should I email the teacher? How will this affect his grade?* She resisted the urge to intervene and simply replied by saying, "Yeah, that's a tough situation." Vinod seemed calmer so Pooja went back to making dinner.

While they were eating, Vinod looked at his mom and said, "My teacher gives so many tests, one bad score shouldn't be a big deal. Besides, I could always do the extra credit project." Pooja smiled at her son and said, "That's the spirit. It's great to see you bouncing back from a hard day." Pooja felt relieved and satisfied. She had provided a soft landing that allowed Vinod to feel safe enough to take responsibility for his actions.

CAN PARENTS LEARN NEW HABITS?

STEP is a reminder that positive change happens incrementally, one step at a time. Research shows that changing behaviors or habits that no longer serve you requires identifying underlying needs and mistaken attempts to meet those needs. This takes introspection, trial and error, and persistence. While we all tend to want to make sweeping changes instantly, a reactive approach often ends in frustration. Change is most effective when it is taken in small, realistic steps, and continually revisited and tweaked until the desired outcome is reached.

We learn from neuroscience that the human brain is able to keep growing and changing throughout our lifetime. This idea of learning and incorporating new concepts and habits is known as plasticity. Adults who focus on learning new skills with meaningful support continue to grow. In fact, research shows the importance of using our brains like a muscle. It's never too late to learn and grow as a parent.

WHAT DOES POSITIVE CHANGE LOOK LIKE?

In *The Power of Habit*, Charles Duhigg explains what neuroscientists have discovered about habits. They are the thousands of things we do on a daily basis with little or no mental effort, such as brushing our teeth, putting on shoes, or backing our car out of the driveway. Researchers discovered that habits comprise a three-part loop, which includes a cue, a routine, and a reward. This important discovery is revolutionary for those seeking positive change. Instead of limiting our focus to the unwanted routine behavior, we now know we need to consider what precedes it (the cue) or ends it (the reward or payoff). These bookends of a habit hold the opportunities for change.

In his book, Duhigg explains how he broke the habit of eating a chocolate chip cookie at 3:00 p.m. on workdays. His pants were uncomfortably tight, and he wanted to cut out unhealthy snacking. It took several attempts to identify the cue and then experiment with alternate rewards that would meet his need. Turns out, his need wasn't food but socialization. Each time he went to the cafeteria to buy the cookie, he would see colleagues and chat with them. Once he identified his need for socializing at 3:00 p.m. (cue), he could replace the cookie-eating habit with going to a colleague's desk to say hello for a few minutes. It took a few weeks of practicing the new habit before he noticed he wasn't thinking about the cookie much anymore. After six months of this new routine, it had become automatic, and he had lost weight. Duhigg's habit met his need for socializing and fit his vision of losing weight.

> Parents who approach change with curiosity and openness have an easier time adopting new parenting habits.

Unsuccessful habits also develop in our relationships and can be changed when we bring attention to the cues and rewards. For example, a child routinely comes home from school and throws down his backpack with a sigh (cue). Mom routinely asks, "How much homework do you have?" In response, the child complains or acts out. While it's not obvious, the reward to the mom may be the relief she feels after asking the question because she believes she is being a responsible parent by reminding the child to do his homework. However, this mother's behavior contradicts her values of building independence and responsibility in her child.

To change the habit, the parent explores options to reinforce a close relationship while allowing her child to be responsible for his homework. She could choose to smile, welcome the child home and delay asking about homework until the child has had a break. Or, the parent could challenge her thinking around the reward. Instead of feeling relief from giving reminders she could focus on helping the child develop responsibility. Whichever option the parent chooses, she is being aware and intentional in her actions. We hope you find relief from Duhigg's findings that "habits are not destiny ... habits can be ignored, changed, or replaced."

TRYING ON NEW HABITS

It takes time and effort to break down a current routine or communication pattern. Our efforts to change need to be intentional and deliberate after considering our present situation and our preferred future. Pay attention to what boosts or drains your energy when deciding what to focus on and considering different options. As Duhigg describes in his cookie story, experimentation is also essential to effective change. Scientists know that a failed hypothesis means there is more learning to be done. Recall the famous words of Thomas Edison: "I have not failed. I've just found 10,000 ways that won't work."

We invite you to think about shifting your current parenting approach as an experiment.

- What's holding you back from living out your vision today?
- Is there a family routine that needs your attention?
- Are there any negative habits you would like to change
  or replace?
- What payoff do you or your child get from the current,
  undesirable habit?
- Is there a different way to meet your needs and/or your
  child's needs in the situation?

- What is your desired outcome for this situation?
- Which new parenting skill are you interested in exploring?
- What support from others do you need to put the desired change in place?

We hope you have identified several growth opportunities to become the parent you want to be for your family. We reiterate the importance of a *Practice for Progress* mindset. Applying new parenting skills may feel awkward. By introducing a new habit, you are interrupting the reactive approach to parenting. Go easy on yourself. Be open to trial and error and tweaking along the way until you find what works best for you and your family.

Take the first step in faith.
You don't have to see the whole staircase,
just take the first step.
Martin Luther King, Jr.

---------------------------**8**---------------------------

ENERGIZING YOUR
ACTION PLAN

In this closing chapter, we invite you to:

- Set realistic expectations for change and celebrate progress
- Find ways to renew and boost your energy
- Add rituals and community support to catalyze your vision

Changing unwanted behaviors and adopting new habits can be confusing and frustrating. The uncomfortable reality is there is no quick fix when it comes to parenting. When parents come back to us saying their self-improvement efforts did not produce the desired results as quickly as they had hoped, we discuss reviewing their expectations. Even when parents use positive skills, the outcome may not be what they hoped. Children may withdraw or act out when parents behave in unpredictable ways. The same is true for co-parents. When disrupting the status quo, things may seem worse before they get better. Productive change takes time, perseverance, and a willingness to experiment.

The road to personal growth is bumpy. We see parents go through ups and downs during the coaching process. Often a parent will tell us, "I worked on the things we discussed last time, but then these three other challenging situations came up in our family." As coaches, our job is to make sure the parent slows down and recognizes positive indicators of progress.

> Parenting well depends on recognizing what's working for you and your family and persevering through chaos and challenges.

We encourage you to keep going through the process of changing from your current situation to what you truly desire for your family. Get to know yourself and your co-parent better. Learn what works for each of you. Align your actions with your priorities and meaningful vision. Stay true to yourself and trust that your daily efforts to achieve your parenting goals will pay off.

STEP OUT OF THE CHAOS

Our children's growth and our own growth as parents proceeds in a wavy, up-and-down line, which can be difficult to observe when we are in the midst of it. We encourage you to Step OUT of the chaos and appreciate the progress you've made since picking up this book. We hope you let go of any perfectionist tendencies you may be clinging to as you navigate your daily life.

In Chapter 7, we introduced the STEP model for making intentional parenting decisions in real time. We also provided a framework for thinking through how to respond to common parenting dilemmas using the Step UP, Step WITH, and Step BACK categories. We now introduce Step OUT, which is focused on your needs and vision as a parent. Parenting is a 24/7 vocation on top of all your other responsibilities. It is an emotional and stressful endeavor even when things are running smoothly. For continued and lasting growth as a parent, we encourage parents to take breaks from the chaos of their daily lives and view their progress from a wider perspective. These moments of self-reflection and appreciation help reset expectations and provide fuel for continued growth.

How do parents Step OUT from the whirlwind of constant demands of caregiving, maintaining a home, and earning a living? In coaching sessions, parents have shared creative ways to care for themselves and stay on course toward achieving their parenting visions. In this chapter, we discuss some popular strategies parents have found helpful. Keep an open mind and explore what resonates with you. Pay attention to your energy level as you test out

Energy is critical for sustaining new habits and refining your personalized approach to parenting well.

different approaches and lean into those which renew or increase your energy.

CELEBRATE YOUR WINS IN REAL TIME

A key strategy we practice and share with parents is to celebrate what's working in real time. Begin by slowing down and taking a wider view of the current situation. This may feel unnatural at first if you are in the habit of worrying, or have trouble staying in the present moment. Humans waste countless minutes ruminating on the past and feeling anxious about the future. We challenge you to pause and consider the here and now. Take a closer look at your daily life, and all of the ways you care for yourself, your family, and your community.

Read through the following questions. You may want to do this activity in the evening as a way to look back on the day. Look for three meaningful things that made you smile or brought a sense of accomplishment.

How did you take care of yourself today? Some examples are:
- Got needed rest
- Drank lots of water
- Ate healthy food
- Took time for prayer or meditation
- Exercised
- Connected with a friend or loved one
- Used positive self-talk

What did you do well today as a parent? Some examples are:

- Said encouraging words to your child
- Refrained from yelling or lecturing
- Upheld a family rule
- Followed through on what you said you would do
- Spent time connecting with your child
- Shared a meal without checking your phone
- Practiced a new habit

What positive trends are emerging from your parenting efforts? Some examples are:

- Less reactive behavior
- More understanding for your child's temperament
- More compassion toward yourself in difficult situations
- More collaboration with your co-parent
- Greater clarity on your desired outcomes
- Less need to compare yourself to others

What positive behaviors are you observing in your child? Some examples are:

- Doing a task independently
- Taking responsibility for a mistake
- Being respectful to you or a sibling
- Following a family rule without complaining
- Talking about feelings

What brought you joy today? Some examples are:

- Got through the morning routine calmly
- Picked up your child from daycare on time
- Saw your children playing together well
- Had an easier time with homework or getting to bed
- Spent time with your spouse/partner

With practice and repetition, this type of daily examination can help you develop greater appreciation for yourself and your loved ones. The goal is to let your efforts in creating and experiencing these positive moments sink in and renew you.

MINDSET MATTERS

Parents who demonstrate a positive mindset have an easier time creating their vision and making their vision a reality. Even in the midst of the old habits and patterns in the family dynamic, willing parents realize they have a choice to do things differently. For some parents, having a positive mindset means being open and curious. For others, it is staying hopeful. Or, it may mean feeling grateful. You may feel grateful for the sun rising and shining and you may feel grateful for your toddler sleeping through the night. You may feel grateful for the smile of a fellow commuter, or your manager acknowledging a job well done. We encourage parents who are frustrated with themselves, their child, or co-parent to find something positive to acknowledge about the other person. Gratitude is a powerful exercise for resetting patterns of interaction and injecting positive energy into a negative family dynamic.

By positive mindset, we don't mean ignoring reality or wearing rose-colored glasses. Positive thinking requires diligent attention. As humans we are hard-wired to look for potential threats as part of our survival instinct. It takes practice to pay attention to what is working well. The good news is the payoff for focusing on the positive is significant. Just as negative emotions drain our energy and can lead to us feeling stuck in an undesirable situation, positive emotions give us a boost and expand our thinking about how to improve our lives. Barbara Fredrickson is a highly acclaimed research professor and author of the groundbreaking book, *Positivity*. She and her colleagues discovered a positivity ratio of 3:1 to strive for in daily life. In other words, people who experience three positive emotions for every one negative emotion are happier and more resilient when faced with adversity.

STRENGTHEN YOUR VISION

After taking a closer look at who you and your child are as individuals in Chapters 1 and 2, we moved to the pillars of parenting in Chapter 3. We introduced three categories of parenting pillars: relationship pillars, teaching pillars, and support pillars to help you prioritize areas for improvement and formulate an authentic action plan. We provided tools and strategies for building the relationship and teaching pillars in Chapters 4 through 6 and introduced the STEP model for responding to everyday situations in alignment with your action plan in Chapter 7.

Now, we turn our attention to the support pillars which include:

- **Self-care:** *Are you committed to be at your best in mind, body and spirit?*
- **Self-awareness:** *Do you pay attention to your inner narrative and what you are thinking and feeling?*
- **Community:** *Do you cultivate a sense of community involvement and support for yourself and your child?*

We know from personal and professional experience the critical importance of these three areas of support for creating and sustaining positive change for individuals, couples, and families. Self-care remains a key practice for parents and caregivers to avoid burnout and to stay in a healthy flow of giving and receiving. Mindfulness is the link to increasing self-awareness. Finding and joining with community — whether that's a group of peers, colleagues, family members, or friends — is another habit we see parents use to meet and exceed their vision. In fact, this trio of parent coaches wouldn't be working together as authors if it wasn't for the supportive community we formed!

STRETCH YOUR VIEW OF SELF-CARE

Self-care provides us with energy to keep moving toward our parenting goals. It teaches our bodies and minds how to relax and reflect. In our coaching work with parents, it is usually one of the first strategies we recommend. We know a mind under stress cannot think as clearly or creatively as a mind that is centered and calm.

When we introduce the STEP model, parents often tell us that the first part—slow down—is the most difficult for them. Is it because we live in such a fast-paced

society where we are driven to be productive and always looking ahead to what's next on our mental to-do list? How can we cue ourselves to slow down, when this action seems foreign to our bodies and brains? We believe the answer is positive self-talk and attention to self-care. By making self-care activities an important priority, we practice slowing down and learn to recognize and access this calmer state when it is needed most in our parenting.

Parents often tell us they don't have time to make self-care a priority in their busy schedules. We encourage them to stretch their view of self-care beyond going to the gym or getting a pedicure. Self-care can bring renewal in micro-moments! Some examples are taking three deep breaths, savoring a cup of tea, watching a funny YouTube clip, lighting a candle, or dancing to a favorite song. Imagine grabbing a few minutes in real time to lovingly care for yourself. These micro-moments add up and boost energy.

PUTTING SELF-CARE INTO REAL-TIME ACTION

Scan through the words in the following chart. Do you have ideas for self-care practices that are not on the list? If so, add them. Choose some activities that appeal to you. Pick one to test out today and a second activity to test out later in the week. Some people find it helpful to schedule fifteen to twenty minutes in their calendar for the activity and/or set a reminder on their phone. The objective is to make self-care a daily or weekly habit.

SELF-CARE IDEAS

○ Garden	○ Call a friend	○ Draw or paint
○ Play with your pet	○ Cuddle with your sweetie	○ Play cards or a board game
○ Practice yoga	○ Write in a journal	○ Cook or bake
○ Play sports	○ Go out for a meal	○ Look at recipes
○ Work out or exercise	○ Visit with friends or neighbors	○ Engage in a hobby
○ Listen to music	○ Soak in a bath	○ Take photos
○ Sing in the car	○ Take a class	○ Tell stories
○ Play hide and seek	○ Read a book or magazine	○ Play an instrument
○ Volunteer for a cause	○ Attend a worship service	○ Read or write poetry
○ Do a puzzle or crossword	○ Try a new hairstyle	○ Do a home project
○ Take a nap	○ Breathe deeply	○ Meditate
○ Get a massage	○ Belly laugh	○ Dance
○ Walk, bike, swim, or jog	○ Watch a video or movie	○ Serve the community
○ Clean or organize	○ Tickle your child	○ Research a topic
○ Plan a trip	○ Do needlework	○ Make a craft
○ Play video games	○ Arrange décor	○ Other

SELF-AWARENESS AND SELF-CARE GO HAND IN HAND

As you improve the ways you give to yourself, notice your experience. What are you learning about yourself as you create new habits?

- How did you feel during and after the activity?
- What did you notice about your energy level?
- Did you interact differently with your child or partner immediately after doing the self-care activity?
- Do you prefer to have an accountability partner for support such as a partner or friend?

SELF-CARE IN ACTION

Jane had two active teenagers when her husband accepted a job in another state. She wanted a divorce. Jane was devastated and scared for how she would manage her finances, home, and single parenting. Even though the children would see their father when he was able to get back to town, Jane was resentful that he seemed to expect her to shoulder the responsibilities of daily parenting without much support. As Jane worked with her parent coach, she became aware of her own needs and committed to self-care. She recalled how much she valued her loyal friend Katie with whom she shared stories and laughter. Jane made a point to invite Katie to join her for breakfast once a week. She asked Katie to remind her to stay true to herself while making necessary financial and legal decisions. As a result, Jane was able to better manage her decisions and keep the children out of the conflict she was having with their father. Jane's friendship with Katie was central to the positive changes in her life. Jane appreciated Katie's support in holding her accountable to her own self-care.

ADD RITUALS TO REINFORCE YOUR VISION

We can build muscle for our parenting journey by adding new rituals that reinforce our vision. Mealtime is a common, often daily activity for many families. It is a natural time to add a new routine that fosters connection among family members. Many families report that making dinner screen-free for both parents and children adds to the connection. Research shows family dinner is linked to many positive health outcomes for children and adolescents, including better grades and lower rates of substance abuse. As the American College of Pediatricians states, "Making the 'Family Table' a priority from an early age can serve as a 'vaccine' against many of the harms that come to children from a hurried lifestyle."

What mealtime rituals does your family have in place? For example, does everyone have a part in preparing the meal or table, or cleaning up afterwards? Do you say a prayer or give thanks before starting the meal? There are many creative ways to build connection and strengthen relationships during mealtimes. Parents have shared:

- Take turns having each family member share one high point and one low point from the day.
- Keep conversations during dinner focused on positive topics — avoid reviewing tasks or to-do lists.
- Play simple games such as Twenty Questions or I Spy.
- Create a story with each person making up one line and saying it aloud. The next person builds on it by adding their own line to the story. Keep going until the story has gone around the table at least twice (or until you can't stop laughing!)
- Discuss a current event from an article or video clip.
- Play a short card game, word game, or puzzle.
- Share your music. Rotate among family members getting to choose, share, and explain what they like about a song to the rest of the family.
- Invite members of your community to join in family meals.

CREATING A MEANINGFUL COMMUNITY

Parents who want to live intentionally and affirm their vision experience many benefits from community engagement. Community provides a sense of belonging for family members. It broadens the family's base of support by sharing responsibilities among parents. For example, a

> Your vision is an anchor to keep you focused on what you truly want for your family.

mom in the midst of a divorce found structure and support from the Boy Scout community. The scout meetings and outings gave her eleven-year-old son a sense of belonging during a difficult time when his family structure was fractured. Community also offers opportunities for fun and connection for all family members. Parents have shared the following ways of creating community:

- Friday night neighborhood potluck where families take turns hosting the gathering
- A church group meal-train for new parents during their first days home with baby
- Mothers with similar-aged children who gather to share and support each other
- Fathers who gather for Saturday morning basketball games
- A community softball league for parents of young children where one parent plays softball, the other parent enjoys conversation, and the children play together
- A group of families who organize donations for a local community shelter

COUSINS' NIGHT IS BORN

 Caleb and Jasmine came to parent coaching because of constant fighting over parenting their teenage son. They realized the tremendous stress their differing opinions on discipline were putting on their marriage.

They both wanted to stay together and were open to exploring new ways to work together in raising their son. We began by looking at each of their parenting profiles and discussed what strengths each of them offered the family. Caleb had a relaxed style. He valued being a provider for his family, his strong faith in God, and being helpful to others. Jasmine was a successful bank manager who valued hard work, clear expectations, and a drive for achievement. Discussing their differences helped them each remember what they loved about one another. It also reminded them of the fun they used to have together when they were new parents and less stressed about their child's future. We discussed their vision for their family, and they came up with the following vision statement: *We combine our different styles to find creative ways to have fun as a family.*

In our next coaching session, we discussed how to bring their vision to life. Caleb and Jasmine acknowledged how hard it could be to appreciate the other's viewpoint and thought spending some time together away from parenting issues could help their relationship. They also identified couples who they admired as parents, who seemed to have grown closer while raising their children. Caleb suggested getting together with his cousin and his wife, who they both respected. Jasmine suggested going on a date night to their favorite Chinese restaurant. We discussed what activities they enjoyed doing together. They both mentioned playing card games with family and friends. Together, Caleb and Jasmine decided on a plan. They would invite Caleb's cousin, Sam, and his wife, Vanessa, over for Chinese take-out and cards. This idea made them both smile.

At our next session, Jasmine shared they had a "cousins' night" at their home. Sam and Vanessa picked up Chinese food and they all enjoyed a fun evening eating delicious food and playing card games until nearly midnight. Caleb appreciated having a relaxed night with another couple who shared their family values. Jasmine noted how wonderful it was to have a fun time around the dinner table; it was a refreshing change from arguing in their home. They both seemed filled with renewed energy as they relayed the decision both couples had made: cousins' night would be a monthly tradition! This was a perfect demonstration of combining their styles to have fun as a family.

KEEP GROWING

When we approach the final session with parents, many tell us they are worried about wrapping up. They question if they will be able to keep the positive momentum going on their own. This is when we remind them of some important takeaways about transformational change and point to specific examples from their own experience. We invite you to do the same. Look back at what you have experienced since picking up this book. We trust you have expanded your self-awareness, deepened your understanding of your child, created a family vision based on a few of the parenting pillars, and tested positive parenting strategies using the STEP process.

Like most parents we coach, we imagine you have had to tweak some aspects of your approach when things didn't turn out as planned. If so, congratulations! That means you are taking action and resetting when needed to stay on course. We remind you that growth does not follow a straight line; while the line slopes upward, it zigzags along the way. The key is to keep going especially when times get challenging.

As you finish this final chapter, we leave you with some key points. Know that chaos is a common part of the change process. Things may feel out of control before they improve. Pay attention to what is working for you and your child in real time. Celebrate your wins and notice your mindset. Review and refine your vision statements and action plan as you go. Practice self-care strategies to renew your energy for the daily grind of parenting. Add rituals that strengthen family relationships and support your values. Surround yourself with supportive people who inspire you to stay true to yourself.

Take a long-range view as you move through each day; it can take years to see the culmination of your efforts. Keep hope alive. Choose your action steps for the present moment. With each parenting STEP you take, you will grow more confident, strengthen your relationship with your child, and bring your vision to life.

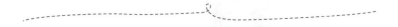

Yesterday is gone.
Tomorrow has not yet come.
We have only today. Let us begin.
Mother Teresa

REFERENCES

Chapter 1: Parenting is About Parents

Baumrind, D. (1967). Childcare practices anteceding three patterns of preschool behavior. *Genetic Psychology Monographs, 75(1),* 43-88.

Kabat-Zinn, J. (1994). *Wherever You Go There You Are: Mindfulness Meditation in Everyday Life.* New York: Hyperion.

Runkel, H. (2007). *ScreamFree Parenting.* New York: Broadway Books.

Siegel, D. & Hartzell, M. (2014). *Parenting from the Inside Out: How a Deeper Self-Understanding Can Help You Raise Children Who Thrive.* New York: Penguin Group.

Tsabary, S. (2010). *The Conscious Parent: Transforming Ourselves, Empowering Our Children.* Vancouver: Namaste Publishing.

Chapter 2: See the Child in Front of You

American Academy of Pediatrics. (2020). Constantly Connected: Adverse Effects of Media on Children & Teens. Retrieved from https://www. healthychildren.org/ English/family-life/Media/Pages/Adverse-Effects-ofTelevision-Commercials.aspx.

American Academy of Pediatrics. (2020). Ages and Stages. Retrieved from https://www.healthychildren.org/english/ages-stages/pages/default.aspx.

DeYoung, C. and Shiner, R. (2013). The Structure of Temperament and Personality Traits: A Developmental Perspective in *Oxford Handbook of Developmental Psychology.* Oxford: Oxford University Press.

Fowler, J; De Neve, J; Christakis, N; Frey B; (2012). Genes, Economics, and Happiness. *Journal of Neuroscience, Psychology, and Economics* Vol. 5, No. 4, 193–211.

National Institutes of Health Genetics Home Reference (2020). Is temperament determined by genetics? Retrieved from https://ghr.nlm.nih.gov/ primer/traits/ temperament.

Hagan, J., Shaw, J., Duncan, P. (2017). *Bright Futures: Guidelines for Health Supervision of Infants, Children and Adolescents, 4th Edition.* Elk Grove Village, IL: American Academy of Pediatrics.

Knight, S. (2016). Technology Trends: When Teens Turn to Social Media for Validation. *Social Work Today* Vol. 16 No. 5 P. 6.

Lickona, T. (1994). *Raising Good Children: From Birth through the Teenage Years.* New York: Bantam Books.

Maker, A. (2018). Screen Time: The Impact on Kids and Parenting. Psychology Today Website. Retrieved from https://www.psychologytoday.com/us/blog/ helping-kids-cope/201808/screen-time-the-impact-kids-and-parenting.

Rock, D. and Siegel, D. (2020). Healthy Mind Platter. Retrieved from https://www.drdansiegel.com/resources/healthy_mind_platter.

Siegel, D. (2014). *Brainstorm: The Power and Purpose of the Teenage Brain.* New York: Penguin Group.

Chapter 3: Creating Your Personal Vision

Hanson, R. and Hanson, F. (2018). *Resilient: How to Grow an Unshakable Core of*

Calm, Strength, and Happiness. New York: Random House.

Moran, J. and Weinstock, D. (2011). Assessing Parenting Skills for Family Court. *Journal of Child Custody.* 8:166–188.

Chapter 4: The Magic of the Parent-Child Relationship

Brackett, M. (2019). *Permission to Feel: Unlocking the Power of Emotions to Help Our Kids, Ourselves, and Our Society Thrive.* New York: Celadon Books.

Center on the Developing Child at Harvard University. (2017). Three Principles to Improve Outcomes for Children and Families. Retrieved from http://www.developingchild.harvard.edu.

Gordon, T. (1970). *Parent Effectiveness Training: The Proven Program for Raising Responsible Children.* New York: Three Rivers Press.

Kabat-Zinn, J. (1994). *Wherever You Go There You Are: Mindfulness Meditation in Everyday Life.* New York: Hyperion.

Milne, A.A. (1928). *The House at Pooh Corner.* London: Methuen Publishing Ltd.

Rosenberg, M. (2015). Nonviolent Communication: *A Language of Life, 3rd Edition.* Encinitas, CA: PuddleDancer Press.

Siegel, D. & Hartzell, M. (2014). *Parenting from the Inside Out: How a Deeper Self-Understanding Can Help You Raise Children Who Thrive.* New York: Penguin Group.

Tobin, M. (1996). *The Art of Positive Parenting.* Columbus, OH: Greyden Press.

Tsabary, S. (2010). *The Conscious Parent: Transforming Ourselves, Empowering Our Children*. Vancouver: Namaste Publishing.

Chapter 5: Influencing Your Child's Behavior

Dweck, C. (2006). *Mindset, The New Psychology of Success*. New York: Ballantine Books.

Faber, A. & Mazlish, E. (1980). *How To Talk So Kids Will Listen & Listen So Kids Will Talk*. New York: Avon Books.

Greene, R. (2001). *The Explosive Child: A New Approach for Understanding and Parenting Easily Frustrated, Chronically Inflexible Children*. New York: HarperCollins Publishers.

Nelsen, J. (1981). *Positive Discipline: The Classic Guide to Helping Children Develop Self-Discipline, Responsibility, Cooperation, and Problem-Solving Skills*. New York: Ballantine Books.

Chapter 6: Discipline Means Teaching Responsibility

Etymonline.com. (2017). *Online Etymology Dictionary*. Retrieved from https://etymonline.com/search?q=discipline.

Nelsen, J. (1981). *Positive Discipline: The Classic Guide to Helping Children Develop Self-Discipline, Responsibility, Cooperation, and Problem-Solving Skills*. New York: Ballantine Books.

Tobin, M. (1996). *The Art of Positive Parenting*. Columbus, OH: Greyden Press.

Chapter 7: Change Happens One STEP at a Time

Duhigg, C. (2012). *The Power of Habit: Why We Do What We Do In Life And Business.* New York: Random House

Kabat-Zinn, J. (2014). What Is Mindful Parenting? Huffington Post. Retrieved from http://www.huffingtonpost.com/jon-kabatzinn-phd/what-is-mindful-parenting_b_5945356.html.

Siegel, D. & Hartzell, M. (2014). *Parenting from the Inside Out: How a Deeper Self-Understanding Can Help You Raise Children Who Thrive.* New York: Penguin Group.

Chapter 8: Energizing Your Action Plan

Anderson, J. and Trumbull, D. (2014). The Benefits of the Family Table. American College of Pediatricians. Retrieved from https://acpeds.org/position-statements/the-benefits-of-the-family-table.

Fredrickson, B. (2009). *Positivity: Discover the Upward Spiral That Will Change Your Life.* New York: Harmony.

ACKNOWLEDGMENTS

The words, stories, and activities included in *Real-Time Parenting* went through many revisions over the years. We are eternally grateful to our editors who generously and diligently offered expert advice. Rachel Clifton, Joe Funari, Chrissie Landolfi, Brian Miller, Julie Peterson, Karen Rafeedie, Sarah Thies, and Kathy Young gave countless hours and helpful suggestions to refine our work. Our hearts are full of appreciation for your significant contributions.

Kristen and Keiji Iwai of KDI Photography skillfully engaged us in conversations to clarify the look and feel of *Real-Time Parenting*. Your encouragement, professional photos, videos, and on-going support gave us confidence to create an authentic product. Thank you for your friendship, professional guidance, and on-going TLC.

We are deeply grateful to The Parent Coaching (PCI) Institute, the world-class parent coach training program, that brought us together as colleagues and friends. We extend our heartfelt thanks to Gloria DeGaetano, the founder of The PCI, for her brilliant work and mission to bring coaching to every parent. Additionally, we want to thank Judy Williams and Action for Children for supporting us as instructors with The Art of Positive Parenting (TAPP) curriculum. TAPP skills are the foundation for the best practices we brought to this writing.

Special thanks go out to our parent coaching mastermind group: Dana Allara, Christine Donovan, Peggy Fitzpatrick, Peggy Gomula, Alice Hanscom, Adrian Kalikow, Cindy Kaplan, and Rhonda Moskowitz. We cherish our memorable times together and so appreciate the commitment to continual learning that brings us together monthly. Your support as fellow coaches keeps us on our toes!

We are delighted to have Tara McGinnis as our esteemed illustrator and layout designer. She is a creative genius! Tara shares our dedication to inspiring parents during the ordinary, challenging, and joyful moments of everyday family life. Big thanks go out to Tara for capturing our ideas in such a lively and light-hearted way.

To all the parents who have shared their heartaches, frustrations, and breakthroughs with us, we are grateful for the trust and partnership we share. Working with parents is a privilege; we are humbled and joyful to be companions on your parenting journey.

Each of us would like to name some additional individuals who propelled our work bringing *Real-Time Parenting* to life.

MARY

Thank you to my friends and family who always asked about our progress with writing this book and never seemed to tire of me sharing the stops, starts, twists, and turns involved in the lengthy process. Your encouragement and support gave me energy to persevere!

Thank you to Cindy, my sister, for caring for me so deeply, modeling how to be a mom to a son, and providing countless hours of loving care to my children when they were young. I cherish the special connection we share!

Thank you to Joe and Chris, my sons, for always cheering me on! Words cannot express the love, respect, and gratitude I feel for each of you. You opened my mind to become more understanding of different learning styles and perspectives. You opened my heart to become vulnerable and accepting of help from others. You opened my soul to become an advocate for children and parents. You inspire me and fill me with joy!

Thank you to Paul, my husband, parenting partner, and champion. You are always supportive of my work and understanding about the many hours I dedicate to it. Thank you for making me laugh, reminding me to appreciate the moment, and modeling resilience. I love you and treasure every day we have together!

BETH

To my family and friends who have been faithful cheerleaders throughout this process — thank you for your encouragement, enthusiasm, and care.

My mother and my sister believe in me wholeheartedly and love me unconditionally. You are forever there for me and for my family. I am forever grateful.

My husband, David, has been by my side for over thirty years. Thank you for your beautiful smile, never-ending support, and enduring love. I am grateful for your partnership on this parenting journey that has deepened our learning and expanded our love. I love and appreciate you!

And to my precious sons, Andrew, Brian, and Christian. Thank you for being my best teachers and greatest inspiration. Watching you grow into lovely, thoughtful, perfectly imperfect young men has been an extraordinary honor and joy. I am grateful beyond words for all the ways you have enriched my life. I love you.

AMY

I am so grateful for my close friends, colleagues, and family who shared in the excitement of writing and publishing this work. My grown children have become trusted friends and dependable supporters. Thank you to Rachel, Olivia, and Ben for your encouragement when I am in self-doubt, and for your grace when I talk too much about my work! This appreciation extends to their spouses Scott, Jacob, and Delilah, and to my stepchildren Trey, Tristan, and Emerson. You graciously remind me that there is no one-size-fits-all parenting and teach me the importance of co-creating family culture. I'm thankful for your warmth and good humor.

At the time of this writing, I also have two adored grandchildren to thank, Calvin and Kacey, who remind me love unfolds in the present moment and each moment is all that matters. You make the phrase "real time" very meaningful!

My husband Edward has graciously been flexible with our time together, granting his support for all the weekends I spent writing. You remind me every day that life is about learning, making others feel loved, and having fun all along the way. I am full of love and gratitude for your patience and partnership.

ABOUT US

BETH MILLER supports parents in creating positive family relationships. With a background in special education and counseling, she helps parents navigate behavior challenges and daily interactions. Beth offers classes and seminars to businesses, schools, and community groups on a variety of topics including effective communication, positive discipline, and work-home balance. Beth enjoys traveling, connecting with friends, and spending time on her yoga mat and paddle board. Beth and her husband live in the Chicago area and have three grown sons.

MARY FUNARI is a resilience coach for working parents. She helps new mothers and fathers gain comfort and confidence in their parenting roles. She facilitates workshops offering practical strategies for managing work and family responsibilities. In addition, Mary is passionate about supporting families with special needs children. A native of Pennsylvania, Mary enjoys long walks in the woods, golf, yoga, and sharing meals and conversation with her family. Mary and her husband have two grown sons.

AMY ARMSTRONG has dedicated her career to creating safe conversational spaces for positive change. She engages mothers and fathers in innovative conflict resolution processes for strengthening co-parenting and family relationships. A native of Columbus, Ohio, Amy is a licensed social worker and trains other professionals in the art of coaching. Outside of her work life, you can find Amy hiking, traveling, and spending time with her family including her husband, three grown children, their spouses, three step-children, and her cherished grandchildren.

TARA MCGINNIS is a busy, stay-at-home mother as well as a freelance designer and illustrator. She enjoys spending quality time with her family, and appreciates learning and implementing *Real-Time Parenting* in her everyday life. Tara resides in Ohio with her husband and two young children.

REAL-TIME PARENTING

CHOOSE YOUR ACTION STEPS FOR THE PRESENT MOMENT

The *Real-Time Parenting* book gives you lots to think about. The expert information, stories, and activities all come together to give you confidence, hope, and new habits.

Want more from us? We are excited to hear from you!

Find us at www.trueparentcoaching.com

Invite us to your next business meeting, conference, school event, podcast, or community group.

Sign up for our next *Real-Time Parenting* class with live interactive instruction and coaching.

Don't miss this chance to put your learning into real-time action!

We are here to guide you in discovering what is true for you!

CPSIA information can be obtained
at www.ICGtesting.com
Printed in the USA
BVHW041213230321
603264BV00014B/228

9 780578 854830